Praise for *Point of Departure: Returning to Our* *for Education and Survival*

Four Arrows provides a quintessential critique of how the c of modern society from "Indigenous Consciousness" has led to the current .... exploitation and destruction of "Indigenous Nature" . . . while providing the impetus for the urgency of a return to the "Indigenous Mind" as one of the true pathways for our future survival.

—**Greg Cajete**
Director of Native American Studies
University of New Mexico
Author of *Native Science* and *Look to the Mountain*

Recognizing the disastrous consequences of the dominant worldview pervading global society, Four Arrows teaches metacognitive strategies to help shift us back toward the Indigenous worldview—the only worldview that can restore balance amidst planetary crisis. With his characteristic insight, he reminds us that interconnectedness with all of creation is the basis of courage that will help each of us, Indigenous and non-Indigenous alike, rise to action in defense of Mother Earth.

—**Waziyatawin**
Dakota author and activist
from Pezihutazizi K'api Makoce (Land Where They Dig for Yellow Medicine)
in southwestern Minnesota

Four Arrows continues to open our eyes to the possibility of a new society, one founded on the empirical data of thousands of years and within the paradigms of traditional wisdom and the people connected to all of life—theirs, ours, animal brethren and Mother Earth. *Point of Departure* is a MUST read for anyone who wants to be part of the solution.

—**Rebecca Adamson**
Founder/President First Peoples Worldwide

With grace and honesty, Four Arrows educates us about human capacities, reminds us about what our ancestors knew and shows us traditional ways to heal ourselves. He gives us faith in the power of humanity's self-transformation, perhaps our greatest hope in these challenging times. Four Arrows inspires us to learn how to be fearless and courageously rejoin the earth community. *Point of Departure* is a welcomed book!

—**Darcia Narvaez**
Professor of Psychology at the University of Notre Dame
Author of *Neurobiology and the Development of Human Morality:*
Evolution, Culture and Wisdom

Courage begins consciousness and here is proof. In this book Four Arrows describes Indigenous tacit knowledge for mainstream society . . . Interconnection is made potent and viable because of its descriptions from *authentic* knowing. We return there now to be of service. Here is the mana of this book—let us learn this together! Ho'oulu lahui o moana-nui-akea.

—**Manulani Aluli Meyer**
Director of Indigenous Education
University of Hawaii West Oahu

Anyone who is even slightly Indigenous will nod in recognition all the way through *Point of Departure*. Using the four sacred directions as cognitive bridges into the circle of all, Four Arrows walks the reader through trance-based, transformative learning; courage, Indian-style, as connection- not fear-based; and the Indigenous grammar of communication and truth-telling, with neither restricted to humans. Then, binding the hoop together for "all our relations," Four Arrows recommends re-acquaintance with Nature. The handy "take-away" discussions and "how-to" manuals concluding each discussion draw the reader into the circle, if only the reader is willing.

—**Barbara Alice Mann**
Associate Professor of Humanities
University of Toledo
Author of *Spirits of Blood, Spirits of Breath: The Twinned Cosmos of Indigenous America*

Point of Departure offers humanity a call to a higher consciousness for a New 21st Century Mind... Four Arrows holds the mirror for every reader to act on his challenge to birth an education system created on praxis of ethical values in a social justice construct, balancing the Natural Laws of the Earth and the supreme universal spiritual laws governing all of humanity.

—**Kahontakwas Diane Longboat**
Turtle Clan, Mohawk Nation
Ceremonial leader and Speaker of the Governing Council of Soul of the Mother

I have lectured on fourth world (Indigenous) concepts of democracy, feminism, environmentalism, and gender fluidity for nearly fifty years. I had little inkling that such thinking would become a new paradigm—indeed, in the environmental realm, a required survival plan. Four Arrows' new book places this thinking in a worldwide context and ought to be required reading in many fields—literature, history, law, anthropology, and cross-cultural communication.

—**Bruce E. Johansen**
Jacob J. Isaacson University Research Professor
School of Communication
University of Nebraska at Omaha

Four Arrows (Don Jacobs)'s *Point of Departure: Returning to Our More Authentic Worldview for Education and Survival* brilliantly calls into question a Western mode of arrogance and dominance that has brought Mother Earth to the brink. He provides much needed and practical insights about the accumulated knowledge and wisdom of nations and peoples with a track record of living in their traditional territories with ecological systems, in perpetuity, prior to the massively destructive onslaught of colonization.

—**Steven Newcomb** (Shawnee, Lenape)
Author of *Pagans in the Promised Land: Decoding the Doctrine of Christian Discovery*

Point of Departure is a powerful and wise prescription for healing ourselves and our planet. With authority and eloquence, it offers a paradigm-shattering opportunity for metacognition work that can move us beyond misperceived limitations so we can write new empowering stories for our lives.

—**Bruce H. Lipton**
Author of *The Biology of Belief*

How will we get beyond our "Western" narcissism to explore, listen, and trust non-dominant cultural discourses which open us to sustainability and yes, survival? This book creates a pathway, reasonably and humanely brings us to a critical consciousness of emancipation and activism. The time is now... to embrace praxis-based ways of knowing and humbly look to Elders of knowledge for nourishment and survival. Four Arrows starts us on the journey.

—**Shirley R. Steinberg**
Research Professor of Youth Studies
University of Calgary and founder, freireproject.org

Point of Departure

Point of Departure

Returning to Our More Authentic
Worldview for Education and Survival

Four Arrows (*Wahinkpe Topa*)
aka Donald Trent Jacobs
Fielding Graduate University

INFORMATION AGE PUBLISHING, INC.
Charlotte, NC • www.infoagepub.com

Library of Congress Cataloging-in-Publication Data

A CIP record for this book is available from the Library of Congress
http://www.loc.gov

ISBN: 978-1-68123-590-5 (Paperback)
        978-1-68123-591-2 (Hardcover)
        978-1-68123-592-9 (ebook)

*I dedicate this text to the Indigenous Peoples who against all odds
are trying their best to hold on to their traditional, Nature-based worldview
and unique tribal place-based cultures; and to all others who are helping them
while at the same time rediscovering and recreating their own Indigenous
selfhood in behalf of future generations of all life on Earth.*

Contents

Who I Am

(About the Author)

I think it important for the reader to know a little about my qualifications for writing a book that claims to describe Indigenous perspectives, whether generalized or specific to a particular tribal culture. The Irish and Cherokee is in my ancestry but I did not feel part of either until after reflecting on a near-death experience in a kayaking accident in Mexico. Then living and Sun Dancing with the Oglala confirmed the importance of my Indigenous inheritance just before I fulfilled my fourth Sun Dance with the Oglala Medicine Horse group. After being brought down from the hill the morning after my preparatory *Hanbleceya*, Rick Two Dogs gave me my name *Wahinkpe Topa* (Four Arrows) based on a vision I shared in the *initi*. Oglala naming, like that of most Plains Indian naming customs, "provides community affirmation of one's new identity, a type of secular and spiritual transformation" (Schubnell, 1997, p. 49). Indeed, in Indian country a man's life proceeds from his name. It adds new dimensions onto previous ones, and a person is expected to live up to his or her name.

As for my Tsalagi (Cherokee) ancestry, Mom mentioned it but mostly when intoxicated and often with mixed emotions. Her father seemed to have been proud of the heritage but had committed suicide. Growing up I had mixed emotions as well. I'll never forget the day Mom brought the Roy Rogers lunchbox I forgot to take to my first-grade classroom. She had rushed to get it to me and had not put on her makeup to cover her

Point of Departure, pages ix–x
Copyright © 2016 by Information Age Publishing
All rights of reproduction in any form reserved.

beautiful Indigenous features. When she left the classroom all the children started chanting "Donnie's mom's a squaw." Mortified, I looked to the teacher for aid. The last thing I saw as I ran out of the school was her sardonic smile. The event stifled my interest in what mathematically amounts to only around 1/32 Cherokee ancestry (in contrast to well over 50% Irish ancestry.) However, "being Indian" has little to do with blood quantum, as the reader may learn.

After my honorable discharge from the Marine Corps in 1969, I spent more than a decade trying to knock a chip of anger off my shoulder with radical outdoor adventure sports, including 100 mile endurance riding, iron man events, dogsled racing, ocean sailing, and white water river kayaking. In 1985, I had a life-changing near-death experience on a kayaking expedition down the Rio Urique deep in Mexico's Copper Canyon. Rescued by local Raramuri Indians, the experience led to a rekindling of my DNA's Indigenous sensibilities. In 1997, I returned to the Raramuri People who saved my life and learned from Raramuri shamans why what happened to me had been so life-changing. This led to my getting an EdD from Boise State University with a cognate in Indigenous Worldview, in which I wrote about the experience later published in a book entitled *Primal Awareness: Survival, Awakening and Transformation with the Raramuri Shamans of Mexico*. In it I introduce an interpretation of a vision I had shortly after the river accident, a vision that uniquely unfolds reveals itself in the new Medicine Wheel I use for this text.

Immediately upon graduation, I accepted a job as dean of education at Oglala Lakota College on the Pine Ridge Reservation. Later I moved on to work with different First Nations at Northern Arizona University where I received my tenure shortly before quitting and moving to Mexico. By the time of my fourth *Owíwaŋyaŋg Wačhí* and the receiving of my Oglala name, I knew my purpose in life was to help people remember our Indigenous roots while doing what we can to help those who have tried to hold on to it.

Preface

*The first thing that's done is you give thanks to everything. You thank the waters
beneath the Earth, the stones, the soil, all the way up to the stars.
It's just a reminder of where we are.*

—Kahionhes John Fadden, Turtle Clan of the Mohawk Nation.

*This is no mere matter for the philosophy classroom. We face the possible
or probable extinction of life on our planet. If we can, we must grasp the bias
and limitations of the "West's" worldview, powered by a hegemony that makes us
oblivious to the wisdom of the people of America's First Nations.*

—Bruce Wilshire

Nature teaches us the importance of finding ways to bring seem-ingly conflicting opposites into harmony without destroying either one. This claim stems from a worldview derived from diverse Indigenous Peoples[1] whose ancestors—also our ancestors—studied nature deeply and holistically for hundreds of thousands of years. There is a second worldview, however, that has emerged during the past nine or ten thousand years that has largely departed from the first one. Is there a way to bring these two conflicting worldviews into harmony? Or is worldview such a foundational concept, unlike culture, ideology, religion, science, or philosophy, that only one of these two worldviews can be said to truly inspire us to strive for such complementarity that will allow us to borrow from both?

Point of Departure, pages xi–xiv
Copyright © 2016 by Information Age Publishing

In this book I propose that we have only these two worldviews operating today.[2] Paradoxically, only our original one can embrace the mandate for seeking complementarity. We may be able to embrace some things that emerged from the more recent and now dominant worldview but without returning to the basic precepts of our original instructions, we will continue to destroy our life systems. Little Bear (2000) explains in his book chapter entitled "Jagged Worldviews Collide," Indigenous worldviews contrast sharply with the dominant worldview. As a result, "many scholars are hesitant to address comprehensive concepts such as worldviews" (Gill 3). Of course, ignoring or dismissing Indigenous worldview "has been and continues to be one of the major tools of colonization" (Walker 531).

An example of the denial of Indigenous worldview is illustrated by a fact that most of us did not learn in our high school civics class, namely that the Haudenosaunee (Iroquois) Confederacy of the Mohawk, Oneida, Onondaga, Cayuga, Seneca and Tuscarora nations "helped shape the political beliefs and institutes of the United States and through it democracy worldwide" (Johansen 46). The founding fathers of the United States borrowed from a political governance system very different from the European ruling hierarchies of the era. A complementarity among opposites occurred, although the same uninvestigated worldview remained operational. As a result, some vital aspects of the Iroquois Confederacy were left out, such as the seventh generation principle, the important role of women, equality among all people, and the honoring of plants and animals via clan systems and ceremony. I believe the consequences of such foundational omissions make my point. As the following pages in this book reveal, the amazing system that emerged was seriously compromised by virtue of having a different worldview—one that is promoting and maintaining insanity—an insanity we must bring back with love and dedication to health.

Even today the Haudenosaunee continue to honor their agreement first made in 1600 to work in harmony with the Europeans who invaded their lands (Ransom & Ettenger). They are committed to partnerships still, but within the parameters of the original worldview. The Haudenosaunee Environmental Protection Process (HEPP) was recently created to work with U.S. federal and state agencies to help restore health to polluted and imbalanced life systems in their territories. However, they are clear that in so doing, they will abide by their original worldview.

> As friends, we are open to share ideas, methodology, and processes that assist each of us to attain our goal: a healthy environment for the "seventh generation." Such codes, however, which are absent of our traditional law

and knowledge, promote assimilation by replacing traditional teachings and principles with federal and state laws.... The HEPP is being developed based on a Haudenosaunee indigenous worldview and relationship with the natural world. (LaFrance & Costello 66)

In order to keep the wisdom of the original worldview at the heart of all decisions, the HEPP members begin and end each meeting with their traditional Thanksgiving Address (*Ohen:ton Karihwatehkwen*). Many also say it as a daily sunrise prayer. It is an ancient message of peace and appreciation of Mother Earth and her inhabitants and is used to express appreciation for life's diversity. Like similar prayers or invocations of most Indigenous cultures, it is used to remind us of all of the relationships and responsibilities that promote health. It creates a natural basis for environmental protection. In the address, people acknowledge each natural and supernatural aspect of the environment with sincere gratitude.

These components are as follows: The People; The Earth, Our Mother; The Plants, Berries, and the Three Sisters; The Waters; The Fishes; The Trees; The Animals; The Birds; The Wind; The Thunderers, Our Grandfathers; The Sun, Our Elder Brother; The Moon, Our Grandmother; The Stars; The Four Beings; and Our Creator. When one recites the Thanksgiving Address, the natural world is thanked, and in thanking each life-sustaining force, one becomes spiritually tied to each of the forces of the natural and spiritual world. The Thanksgiving Address teaches mutual respect, conservation, love, generosity, and the responsibility to understand that what is done to one part of the Web of Life, we do to ourselves (LaFrance & Costello).

I know that such sentiments as conveyed here will resonate with most readers because the Indigenous worldview remains in all of our hearts. How we can return to it in practical, meaningful ways is the offering I hope to provide with the following pages. Let us begin with the closing stanza of the Thanksgiving Address (Smithsonian National Museum of the American Indian, 1993):

We have now become like one being, with one body, one heart, one mind. We send our Prayers and special Thanksgiving Greetings to all the unborn Children of all the Future Generations. We send our thoughts to the many different Beings we may have missed during our Thanksgiving. With one mind we send our Thanksgiving and Greetings to all of the Nations of the World.

Now our minds are one.

Notes

1. The United Nations Working Group for the Decade of the World's Indigenous People adopted this terminology, using capital letters as a gesture of respect in the same way one might refer to an English or German or European person.
2. Later I will explain the difference between worldviews, beliefs, ideologies, religions, cultures, values, etc.

Reference

Smithsonian National Museum of the American Indian (1993). *Thanksgiving address: Greetings to the natural world.* Retrieved from http://nmai.si.edu/environment/pdf/01_02_Thanksgiving_Address.pdf

Foreword

Bruce Lipton

Every physical object manifests its own unique, invisible force. While an atom appears as a physical particle, we now know that it is comprised of evanescent units of energy called quarks, which are themselves made up of smaller quanta of energy. Rocks, air, water, and humans are all fields of energy that wear the cloak of matter, which makes the old, Descartian notion that the mind (energy) and body (matter) are separate an antiquated anachronism. Such scientific discoveries return us to our aboriginal roots and a worldview that emphasizes our oneness with nature. Indigenous People recognize and honor the "spirits" of the planet, its plants and animals, and the spiritual nature of themselves. Fortunately, many of the lost traditions of our ancestors are still available in the remaining Indigenous cultures and individuals from around the world who have managed to hold on to their traditional knowledge. They still know the wisdom that guided humanity in relatively harmony for most of our time on this planet.

Such wisdom resides deep inside our own DNA, and with the help of those like Four Arrows we can reclaim our original understanding of our place in the world. We do not have to shed our technologies nor abandon our cities to learn again ways to live with local Indigenous knowledge and create relationships with all that can bring us back into harmony with Earth before more species go extinct, including our own. With the ideas

Point of Departure, pages xv–xvi
Copyright © 2016 by Information Age Publishing

presented in this book, Four Arrows helps us to regain our sanity. With a deep understanding of both dominant Western ways of thinking and the contrasting beliefs shared by most of the great variety of Indigenous cultures, he is a veritable modern-day sage offering a visionary approach to remembering who we really are. *Point of Departure: Returning to Our Authentic "Worldview" for Education and Survival* is an important contribution that provides specific strategies to help us relearn the original instructions for living in balance with the Earth. While others have recognized that the solution to our global crises lies in our ancient Indigenous worldview, Four Arrows' synthesis provides valuable insights and specific ways to relearn some of our original instructions in ways that can help mitigate our planetary crises.

Point of Departure is a powerful and wise prescription for healing ourselves and our planet. With authority and eloquence, it offers a paradigm-shattering opportunity for metacognition work that can move us beyond misperceived limitations so we can write new empowering stories for our lives. It guides us out of the current darkness to the light of a consciousness-based spontaneous evolution by bringing us back to the future. Returning to the wisdom that existed before the largely misguided point of departure he describes, we have a chance for a new positive point of departure in behalf of the seventh generation. As you comprehend the enormous potential for applying this information, you will also inspire your spirit, engage your mind, and challenge your creativity.

Bruce H. Lipton, PhD
Author of *The Biology of Belief, The Honeymoon Effect*
and, with Steve Bhaerman, *Spontaneous Evolution*

Introduction

*All humans have a two million year-old person inside and if we lose contact
with that part of us, we lose our real roots.*

—Carl Jung[1]

*The grim prognosis for life on this planet is the consequence of a few centuries
of forgetting what traditional societies knew and the surviving ones still recognize.*

—Noam Chomsky[2]

Worldview Reflection

Expanding on Carl Jung's observation in the quote above, Paul Shepard,
another of the most profound and original thinkers of our time, wrote *Coming Home to the Pleistocene*. He died shortly after writing it and his wife Florence edited it and Island Press published it in 1998. In it he writes,

> When we grasp fully that the best expressions of our humanity were not invented by civilization but by cultures that preceded it, that the natural world
> is not only a set of constraints but of contexts within which we can more fully
> realize our dreams, we will be on the way to a long overdue reconciliation
> between opposites which are of our own making. (Shepard p. 3)

Point of Departure, pages 1–23
Copyright © 2016 by Information Age Publishing
All rights of reproduction in any form reserved.

He goes on to say we do not have to return to the explicit life of a hunter gatherer, but rather we can select those things "under which our genome itself was shaped and incorporate them as best we can by creating a modern life around them" (Shepard 4).

In this book I have selected what I have come to believe are five of the most important "things" to which he refers, understandings that are at the heart of the great variety of Indigenous cultures. I describe specific approaches for understanding and employing them on behalf of personal and planetary transformation. They are precepts of an " Indigenous worldview" that contrasts sharply our "dominant worldview" that currently guides most practices and policies. Using a Medicine Wheel orientation, I focus on "reconciling" these differences as they relate to:

- Trance-based learning
- Fear, courage, and fearlessness
- External authority and self-authority
- Communicative expressions (language and art)
- Engagement with the natural world

One of the many common concepts shared across most Indigenous cultures that forms the Indigenous worldview is the circle. Indigenous worldview holds that humans take many trips around the Medicine Wheel until experiential knowledge moves through self-reflection towards insight into deeper and deeper truths and transformation. I believe this particular version may be one of the most effective metacognitive tools for helping people authentically returning to Indigenous worldview implementation in daily life today.

Without an awareness of our "baseline worldview," well-intended efforts to address global problems will fail to meet our highest mutual goals. Such metacognitive work about why we think what we think about many aspects of one's self and life must start with making conscious our unconscious assumptions buried within our worldview. "Worldview plays a major role in addressing our highly complex, multifaceted, interwoven, planetary sustainability issues" (Hedlund-de Witt 3). It is difficult to employ metacognitive reflection about one's worldview, however, without comparing it to one that is significantly different. To solve this problem, a number of scholars are contrasting the dominant worldview with Indigenous worldview, understanding them as two functioning and historically observable options. By so doing, attention to Indigenous worldview is slowly moving beyond centuries of anti-Indian propaganda, genocide, and hegemony used to support the dominant worldview (Four Arrows). The result is that more and more people are beginning to understand the advantages of a way of understanding the world that guided human behavior for "99%" of human history (Narvaez 643). Tarnas, for example, writes:

> Worldviews create worlds...what sets the modern (worldview) apart is its fundamental tendency to assert and experience a radical separation between subject and object, a distinct division between the human self and the encompassing world. This perspective can be contrasted with what has come to be called the primal worldview, characteristic of traditional indigenous cultures. (16)

The word "worldview" does not adequately describe the deep assumptions held in common by the many diverse Indigenous cultures, but it may be the closest English word available. One of my contributing authors in a book I edited in 2006 makes this point:

> The first thing to be pointed out is the "worldview" is a European idea...So we must recognize initially that in speaking of an Indigenous worldview we may have already generated an egregiously distorted account, determined in advance by a European bias that gives priority to seeing and vision. (Wilshire 261)

Nonetheless, I continue to use the word as it is the best one I know that is available in the English language. We must work with what we have. It works better than just referring to thinking because it points to that which forms our thinking. Einstein's famous truism that we cannot solve problems with the same thinking that caused them is more true when it relates to worldview and not to the thinking, ideologies, religions, and so on that are born from it.

Another concern about the emphasis on Indigenous worldview is related to its pan-Indian orientation. Generalizations about common assumptions held by diverse Indigenous nations can diminish the individual tribal identity. After all, being Indigenous means living in accord with the understandings gleaned from unique local landscape and the life it contains. So how can there be a single worldview when there are so many different geographies? The answer is that a single worldview *does* operate commonly throughout traditional Indigenous cultures in spite of their diversity, just as varied landscapes share common features. If cultural diversity is honored, recognizing a common worldview can bring solidarity and support it. The fact that common features of many Indigenous nations contrast with those among diverse "non-Indian" cultures is potentially useful for everyone's decolonizing efforts.[3]

Although too many world leaders in politics, business, science, and education continue to ignore, dismiss, ridicule, or romanticize Indigenous People and their knowledge, more writers are beginning to recognize that a solution to our ecological crises lies in our ancient Indigenous worldview. Unfortunately, too few writers offer specific solutions. In spite of recognizing the benefits of traditional ecological knowledge, land management and development engineers seldom prioritize it in their work (Hufana). Meanwhile, Indigenous People worldwide are fighting to protect the earth's last pristine geographies. It is not coincidental that the most biodiverse places on our planet are Indigenous territories, as they see "natural resources" as their "relatives." Until all of us can sincerely understand this, we will keep losing ground (no pun intended) and corporations will continue to confiscate the planet's last pristine places. In order to rebalance world systems, an effective solution starts with realizing why we believe what we believe. Fleming writes that metacognitive work is the "key to higher achievement in all domains" (Fleming 31). Authentic self-reflection on conscious and unconscious processes is a vital and seldom-used tool for adjusting our beliefs to manifest healthier outcomes (Lou 121). Returning to our pre point of departure wisdom can help us decide what to take with us on our journey and what to leave behind. This book presents specific metacognitive strategies that can help us to relearn our original instructions for how to live in balance on this Earth.

▬▬

Just Two Worldviews?

I propose that there are only two worldviews: Indigenous and dominant.[4] Most academics resist this idea. They use worldview to describe religions, cultures, and moral beliefs. Many scholars, philosophers, and psychologists have incorrectly viewed humanism, postmodernism, nihilism, existentialism, and many other "isms" as worldviews. Hedlund-de Witt's research tends to support my claim that worldview is much different than these other concepts:

> The concept of worldview may appear to be similar or even interchangeable with concepts such as ideology, paradigm, religion, and discourse, and they indeed possess some degree of referential overlap. However, worldviews can nonetheless be clearly distinguished from these concepts. (Hedlund-de Witt 19)

Robert Redfield, the pioneering social anthropologist from the University of Chicago, adds:

> Worldview differs from culture, ethos, mode of thought and national character. It is the picture the members of a society have of the properties and characters upon their stage of action. Worldview attends especially to the way a man in a particular society sees himself in relation to all else. It is the

properties of existence as distinguished from and related to thee self. It is in short a man's idea of the universe. (Redfield 30)

Redfield valorized the Indigenous worldview of mutuality and cooperation with all without romanticizing it. He believed that what I call our "point of departure" from our Indigenous worldview was a major transformation of human consciousness. It represented to him a devolution from a moral order that bound all life together. According to Redfield, civilization's radical departure from the Indigenous worldview was a cultural invention that resulted in

the loss of a unified, sacred and moral cosmos and its replacement by a thoroughly fragmented, disenchanted and amoral one ... In the primitive worldview man was part of nature and god and acted out of this sense of participation. But gradually man comes to stand aside and look first at God-Nature, then, God-without-Nature, and then, beginning with the Ionian philosophers ... at nature without God.' (p. 109)

Redfield and many scholars who have followed him view Indigenous worldview as a constructive basis for critiquing the dominant modern stance. Knowing that the latter historically tires to destroy or dismiss the former, they also know that they exist as polar opposites that call for comparing and contrasting in ways that help us understand which of each to take with us into the future.[5]

▬
Point of Departure Theory

The point of departure from our relatively harmonious and healthy Nature-based existence to a more anthropocentric and hierarchal one led to the creation of an extremely destructive worldview that has brought us to the dire circumstances we now face. By showing that it is in our nature to live more sustainably and peacefully than the dominant worldview allows, and reclaiming some specific Indigenous understandings about being in the world, we can rebalance our life systems. No one knows exactly when or where to locate the point of departure from our original worldview, but my version of the story follows:

Less than ten thousand years ago, after living for millions of years in relative harmony with earth's life systems, some humans chose to disregard the old ways. Perhaps this occurred when they were especially successful in agriculture, and upon seeing the potential power of a surplus, they became greedy and hoarded a surplus. Maybe a single, strong and charismatic leader simply took over. Whatever the reason, they moved away from the cooperative laws of Nature and adopted a human-centered orientation. Small scale farming that had long been practiced in small ways gave way to farming striving for profitable and power-giving surplus. This led to a few individuals with a high degree of control over many. This transition to a concentration of power culminated in a phenomenon of social transformation when the Akkadians created history's first empire in Northern Mesopotamia (near modern day Syria/Turkey/Iraq) around 7,000 to 9,000 years ago.[6] Having lost their natural grounding in reciprocity and egalitarian life, human societies continued practices that moved further and further away from primal wisdom. Anthropocentrism, religious dogma, absolute rule, class hierarchy, military expansion, slavery, land ownership, economic debt, domination of women, greed, jealousy, a centralized system of government (the state), and large-scale war became the norm. We abandoned our emphasis on interconnectedness and cooperation, forcefully controlled and likely entranced[7] by a dynamic that emphasized dog-eat-dog competition and an arrogant superiority over Nature and each other. We even developed languages to help support and propagate the new worldview.

Although our ancient wisdom has been struggling to survive in the face of progressively disappearing Indigenous languages, lands, and cultural traditions, it still thrives today in a number of Indigenous Peoples. It also lives in the consciousness of people in non-Indian cultures who remember it and try to implement it in varying degrees. If we bring awareness to such innate resources, we might have a chance to regenerate our ability to live on the Earth and survive. This requires us to help existing Indigenous Peoples while borrowing from their wisdom until we can recreate our own Indigenous perspectives related to the places we now inhabit.

Consider how the following Indigenous worldview assumptions differ from the dominant one under which most of us live. I briefly offer the follow Indigenous worldview precepts and, in parenthesis, offer dominant worldview precepts that contrast. (People in dominant worldview oriented cultures can still harbor some Indigenous worldviews and people in Indigenous dominated cultures may have been conditioned to assume dominant worldviews.)

- Life is a complexity of ever-moving, cyclical interactions and relationships that seek harmony (rather than a linear developmental progression of evolution).
- Individual autonomy is prized for his ability to help assure the greater good (as opposed to prizing individualism over community).
- Kinship systems that include the animal/plant world/spirit world extend into the cosmos but are essentially place-based around a particular landscape (instead of being unbound to local landscape and exclusively human oriented).

- Non-human entities including plants, animals, insects, birds, fish, rocks, trees, rivers, celestial bodies, etc., are imbued with spirit/ soul/intelligent energy (whereas in dominant culture these are more likely attributed only to humans.)

- Nature is law, teacher, and the primary relationship (and not that which is only a complex of utilitarian resources for the use of humans or a series of forces to fear and avoid.)

- Metaphysical understandings about Creation although storified in diverse mythologies assign the idea of great dynamic mysterious energies that have generously set us on a path of self-discovery and the challenges of maintaining harmony and interconnectedness (rather than a knowable, personified concept of a single God who has set forth specific rules for behavior and belief.)

- A fearless trust in the universe comes from a continual cultivation of courage and generosity and is grounded in present experience and a continual quest for promoting reciprocity, respect and responsibility in all relationships (whereas fear avoidance and a focus on materialistic gain largely defines the underlying motivations in dominant worldview oriented cultures.)

- Individual health reflects relationships in the world and balance between the relational, mental, spiritual, physical, and emotional (and is not dependent on external expertise of professionals.)

- The highest authority for decision-making is personal reflection on lived experience in the light of a sense of interconnectedness (rather than an external authority figure.)

- Complementarity between most apparent opposites is known to define life systems and is a major philosophical pursuit in the effort to maintain harmony. Bringing offenders back into community employs this understanding (rather than punishment and an emphasis on difference.)

- Language reflects and encourages a focus on motion, transformation, landscape, relationship, subjectivity, and multi-faceted truthfulness (instead of permanence, materialism, objectivity, and deception.).

- Trance-based learning involving alternative consciousness and brain-wave frequencies is fully and continually embraced in concert with both keen observation of the physical world and intuitive engagement with the invisible world of spirit (in contrast with a stronger dependence and focus on reason alone.)

Dr. Darcia Narvaez writes in a prospectus for a book that may publish papers from a conference on Indigenous wisdom at the University of Notre

TABLE I.1 Comparison of Two Types of Living		
	Small bands of Gatherer-Hunters	**United States Today**
Social embeddedness	High	Low
Social support	High	Low
Socially purposeful living	Normative	Non-normative
Community social enjoyment	Every day	Rare (spectator sports, religious services)
Boundaries	Fluid, companionship/kinship culture	Rigid kinship culture, social classes
Physical contact with others	Considerable (sleep, rest, dance, song)	Minimal (only during sleep, child care, greetings)
Relations with other groups	Cooperative	Competitive attitude, cooperative action
Individual freedom	Extensive, no coercion	Free to make consumption choices if adult, coercion
Relationships	Egalitarian, respectful, non-hierarchical	Hierarchical, often disrespectful
Contact with other ages	Multi-age group living day and night	Rare outside of family home
Role models	Virtuous, frequent contact	Often violent or deceptive within popular media

Source: Narvaez (645), used with permission.

Dame in September 2016: "What accounts for the differences between dominant global modern culture and the culture of successful, sustainable indigenous communities that existed for tens of thousands of years?" Her table (Table I.1) shows why we have failed to get our priorities right under the dominant worldview.

Leaky and Lewin's research in *Origins* and in *People of the Lake*, supports this comparison. They write that for around three million years of human history, cooperation was likely the most important original social mandate. Axelrod concurs in his book, *The Evolution of Cooperation*. Darwin might also have agreed, since he mentions "mutual aid" more often than he mentions "competition" in his book, *Descent of Man*. He also writes that human virtues are more important than survival of the fittest.

Anti-Indianism

Due to anti-Indianism, most people probably would not acknowledge that the Indigenous worldview provides a major solution for personal, social,

and planetary survival.[8] Unfortunately, like many other influential thinkers since Socrates[9] who are responsible for maintaining today's dominant
worldview, Darwin promoted an anti-Nature/anti-Indigenous philosophy.
In spite of his scientific insights, he was captive to the dominant paradigm
and without substantive research, believed a questionable informant. He
described his view of an Indigenous person, referring to a Feugian native
he briefly encountered as one who "delights to torture his enemies, offers
up bloody sacrifices, practices infanticide without remorse, treats his wives
like slaves, knows no decency and is haunted by the grossest superstitions."[10]

Such anti-Indianism explains why Indigenous values and beliefs have not
been used as behavioral baselines in efforts to stop climate change, reduce
war, and promote social/ecological justice. Johan M. G. van der Dennen explains this phenomenon in his doctoral dissertation and book entitled *The
Origin of War: The Evolution of a Male-Coalitional Reproductive Strategy*:

> Peaceable preindustrial (preliterate, primitive, etc.) societies constitute a
> nuisance to most theories of warfare and they are, with few exceptions, ei-
> ther denied or 'explained away.' In this contribution I shall argue that the
> claim of universal human belligerence is grossly exaggerated; and that those
> students who have been developing theories of war, proceeding from the
> premise that peace is the "normal" situation, have not been starry-eyed uto-
> pians. (van der Dennen 2)

Even when anti-Indianism is covert, most non-Indigenous people view
life through the lens of our dominant worldview. Greg Cajete, John Lee,
and I expose this problem via neuropsychology in our text, *Critical Neurophilosophy and Indigenous Wisdom*. We found that the conclusions in scientific
studies about concepts such as generosity, honesty, spirituality, courage, and
humility using observed psychological experiments, psychometrics, and advanced brain screening technologies were significantly biased by dominant
worldview assumptions. For example, if an MRI showed part of the brain
activating when people practiced some form of generosity in an artificially
induced experiment, some scientists concluded that generosity is always
self-serving. They held this view because the activation point seemed to be
in the same location where activation for selfish acts occurred. Without the
dominant worldview lens, the scientists might have considered the complexities of consciousness, and they might not come to their conclusion.
They might have considered thousands of years of Indigenous observation
of the natural world relating to generosity, but they were insufficiently exposed to this wisdom, if at all.

Most people assume that we must use the "civilized" wisdom of the
past several thousand years as a baseline to establish future goals for solving

problems. We have been led to believe that "primitive" humans were and are collectively more:

1. warlike
2. brutal with women
3. cruel to children
4. "Godless" and superstitious
5. inhumane
6. oppressive
7. undemocratic
8. harmful to ecosystems
9. unhappy
10. poor in quality of life and health

However, research in all of the above domains shows the opposite is true. These ten traits more accurately describe "civilizations" after the point of departure. A significant body of evidence supports this, but one has to search through the fog of anti-Indian media, education, and folklore to find it. "Academic" publications that reach the general public are easier to access, such as:

- *The Invented Indian* (1990) by James Clifton, who writes that acknowledging anything positive in the native past is a wrongheaded proposition, because no genuine Indian accomplishments have been substantiated.
- *Sick Societies: Challenging the Myth of Primitive Harmony* (1992) by UCLA anthropologist Robert Edgerton, who tries to prove the superiority of Western culture by writing about child abuse and other social maladies he claims (falsely) were more pervasive in primitive societies.
- Lawrence H. Keeley's *War Before Civilization* (1997), proposing that civilization and centralized governments have overcome the horrors of primitive life.
- Robert Whelan's *Wild in the Woods: The Myth of the Peaceful Eco-Savage* (1999), asserts that "Indigenous peoples have little to teach us about caring for the environment."
- Shepard Krech's *The Ecological Indian: Myth and History* (2000), states that the demise of the buffalo was caused by the Indians.
- Steven A. Lablank's *Constant Battles: The Myth of the Peaceful, Nobel Savage* (2003) concludes that technology and science have put mankind on the right trajectory for world peace compared to the barbaric behaviors of aboriginal people.

- Steven Pinker's *The Better Angels of our Nature: Why Violence Has Declined* (2011), uses exaggerated, erroneous stories about Indigenous violence against European colonists to argue that we are better off now than in pre-state societies.

Even Drury and Clavin's *The Heart of Everything that Is* is a New York Times best-selling historical text praised by book reviewers as an accurate depiction of the Lakota and other American Indian tribes. However, it is full of erroneous anti-Indian writing that I exposed in a *Truthout* publication entitled "The Continuing Saga of Anti-Indianism in America."

Regardless of these challenges, if we attempt to identify and go beyond or complement the modern dominant worldview with comparative reflections, we could add proven historical methods to establish achievable actions for human and ecological wellness.[11] Recognizing and implementing the ancient pre-departure beliefs will enable us to understand that we are truly connected, and allow us to realize peace, respect, and sustainability again for the benefit of all human and non-human beings. It would be a mind shift from mutually assured destruction to mutually assured survival. We might start this process of creating realistic goals by looking at the ten social problems listed above; research shows that when we operated under our Indigenous worldview, we fared much better. Deeply acknowledging these facts might enable us to aim much higher.[12] Knowing that it is human nature to be cooperative, peaceful, sustainable, and happy in spite of the past 5,000 to 10,000 years of Western history is vital to regaining our balance.

Challenges for the Reader

Romanticizing the Indigenous

In addition to overcoming the educational and cultural hegemony of anti-Indians, there are other challenges for the reader who seriously engages the ideas in this book. One relates to the common allegation of "romanticizing" the Indigenous. Akin to being called "a conspiracy theorist,"[13] such language can silence people or prevent them from an open-minded reconsideration of facts. David Abram rebuts such accusations in his award-winning book, *Becoming Animal*:

> There are many intellectuals today who feel that any respectful reference to indigenous beliefs smacks of romanticism and a kind of backward-looking nostalgia. Oddly, these same persons often have no problem "looking backward" toward ancient Rome or ancient Greece for philosophical insight and guidance in the present day. What upsets these self-styled "defenders

of civilization" is the implication that civilization might have something to learn from cultures that operate according to an entirely different set of assumptions, cultures that stand outside of historical time and the thrust of progress. (267)[14]

Recognizing Educational and Cultural Hegemony

Related to buying into anti-Indianism, a lack of awareness of educational and cultural hegemony continues to solidify our dominant worldview. As the mixed-blood Cherokee entertainer Will Rogers once said, "It isn't what we don't know that gives us trouble, it's what we know that ain't so." How American educators teach students about Helen Keller is a classic example of hegemony. Due to the control of curriculum by those "in power," few people learn the truth about Keller's amazing history as a socialist who criticized capitalism, became a member of the International Workers of the World and an ardent supporter of labor unions, and also was an outspoken opponent of war. This exemplifies of how the ruling corporate elite minimize heroes who are pro-union, anti-war, or critical of capitalism. Peaceful coexistence and respect for all life forms does not serve the interests of those who have created the dominant global political structures in the past several thousand years. Such hegemony also includes institutionalized acceptance of authoritarian, centralized political systems and the illusion of authentic democracy.[15]

The ultimate way to counter such hegemony and neoliberal assumptions[16] is to learn how to manifest a deep Indigenous understanding about the themes addressed in the following chapters. The reader can learn to re-embrace our legacy of Indigenous wisdom that some First Nations have maintained and that exists within our DNA. Our worldview, not our technologies, can save us. Elias states that:

> One cause of the troubles afflicting the contemporary world is the quality of mind that we have perfected in European American cultures. We have perfected mental capacities that produce technological wonders accompanied by runaway ecological and social crises. If a problem cannot be solved with the type of thinking that created it, the most fruitful way to resolve these dilemmas simply may be to change the way we think. (Elias 44)

Concern About Misappropriating Indigenous Spirituality

You might also be concerned about wrongly appropriating Indigenous ideas or identity. Some Indigenous individuals trying desperately to protect their ways of knowing from being misappropriated will challenge your rights to Indigenous knowledge or practices. I remember when I used part of a tribal ceremony to help implement Indigenous worldview and was scolded for it. When musically entertaining a group of parents at a mostly Navajo school where I served as a board member, I played a Lakota thank-you song usually sung at the end of an *inipi* ceremony. Immediately, a Navajo medicine person came up to me, shook his head and said I should know better than to take the song out of the lodge. Shortly after, another medicine man walked up to me and thanked me for having done so. Indian Country is divided, but I ask you to avoid this. We must understand the pain and politics behind our division, while realizing that we are all in the same boat, which is sinking. We share the legacy of our ancestry and our roots in Grandmother Earth. If you maintain authentic respect, avoid profiting from any Indigenous representation and support Indigenous rights and activism while standing against genocidal forces, you cannot go wrong in re-embracing Indigenous traditions, even if you have not mastered the "protocols."

This does not mean we should not empathize with those who are worried about misrepresentation or misuse of tribal practices, as there are longstanding reasons for protecting protocols that keep traditional ceremonial realities secret, "in the circle," even removed from non-Indians. Misappropriation of spirituality and ceremony has followed the theft of children, land, and dignity. In an effort to counter this, Wilmer Mesteth, Darrell Standing Elk, and Phyllis Swift Hawk wrote a document entitled "War against Exploiters of Lakota Spirituality." Written in the summer of 1993 and signed by many Lakota, Nakota, and Dakota Nation representatives, it tried to stop the commercialization and "New Age" use of traditional ceremonies and the "absurd public posturing of this scandalous assortment of pseudo-Indian charlatans, 'wannabes,' commercial profiteers, cultists and 'New Age shamans' [that] comprises a momentous obstacle in the struggle of traditional Lakota people for an adequate public appraisal of the legitimate political, legal and spiritual needs of real Lakota people."

In 2003, Arvol Looking Horse, the Lakota keeper of the Sacred White Buffalo Calf Pipe, delivered another proclamation to protect Lakota ceremonies from exploitation. In it, he proposed prohibiting non-Indians from participating in Lakota ceremonies. He wrote that anyone who pours water for an *inipi* ceremony must meet certain qualifications; however, a number of spiritual leaders disagreed. Tom Kanatekeniate Cook, a Wolf Clan Mohawk married to a Lakota from Pine Ridge, offered a formal rebuttal "in behalf of the elders of the Afraid of Bear/American Horse Sun Dance in the Black Hills." In *The Appropriation of Native American Spirituality* by Suzanne Owen, Cook quoted Chief American Horse in 1896: "Anyone may dance the sun dance if he will do as the Oglalas do." Cook also pointed out the meaning of the Lakota prayer used when entering and exiting the ceremonial lodge, *mitakuye oyasin* ('all my relations').

I agree with American Horse that Indigenous worldview is a mandate for all inhabitants of Mother Earth; I hope you will re-embrace it before it is too late. Moon-walking astronaut and founder of the Institute of Noetic Sciences, Edgar Mitchell says on the back of John Perkins's book, *Shapeshifting: Techniques for Global and Personal Transformation*, "Only a handful of visionaries have recognized that Indigenous wisdom can aid the transition to a sustainable world." I hope with this book to create many more visionaries!

Personal Identity Claims

Closely related to the cultural misappropriation concerns are sensitivities about how a "non-Indian" identifies as someone embracing Indigenous worldview. Individuals living as Indigenous Peoples worldwide suffer from identity crises. The causes for these crises include discrimination, historical trauma, disempowerment, loss of place, and many others. As a result, many Indigenous people and their supporters are wary of those who seem to pretend to be Indian. But in a sense, my goal in this book is to get everyone to "be Indian" again. There will likely be challenges in assessing the difference between this concept, and the disrespect, ignorance, or thoughtlessness that often accompany "playing Indian." Philip J. Deloria addresses this in his book *Playing Indian*, explaining that although most Americans who donned Indian costumes or practiced their ceremonies did not resolve their contradictions and allowed them to evade real change, it helped others to realize the truth (184). "Creativity is exactly what was so compelling about playing Indian . . . It was a quest for a meaningful freedom and a contingent truth" (185).

A controversial solution to this dilemma is to realize that all of us are indigenous to the planet. Most of us, "full-blood" Indigenous People included, are admixtures of many so-called "races." With this awareness and an understanding of worldview and our point of departure from it, we can dedicate ourselves to preserving Indigenous cultures struggling to survive, while learning to re-embrace thinking that can return us to being Indigenous in our communities. If the heart is sincere and a oneness-oriented worldview is practiced authentically, how you are in the world has as much, or more to do with being Indigenous than blood quantum, genetics, or haplogroup typing. Such identity markers stem from early racist practices fostered by anthropologists and others.[17] Under the dominant worldview, they become competitive and alienating. I agree with N. Scott Momaday who writes that at the most fundamental level, what we imagine ourselves to be and a commitment to a certain set of values and a history of paying one's dues are sufficient to "be Indian" (Jacobs). This idea is presented in Kiowa scholar Perry Horse's third and fourth criteria for creating American Indian self-identity "consciousness":

1. the extent to which one is grounded in one's Native American language and culture, one's cultural identity
2. the validity of one's American Indian genealogy
3. the extent to which one holds a traditional American Indian general philosophy or worldview (emphasizing balance and harmony and drawing on Indian spirituality)
4. one's self-concept as an American Indian
5. one's enrollment (or lack of it) in a tribe (65)

Concerns About Binary Thinking

Another challenge in contrasting the two worldviews comes from those who rightly understand that binary thinking is a dominant worldview problem that Indigenous worldview avoids. My colleague, David Abram, author of *Becoming Animal,* recently wrote to me about my approach to writing about "good and bad" worldviews. He said he did not trust the binary logic and thinks it is destroying our world. I agree, and am trying to point out that such logic dangerously pervades our dominant worldview. He prefers to think of the problems manifested by dominant and untoward actions in the world as being a kind of subset of the only authentic rationale worldview possible (Indigenous). He writes, "My strategy is often to nest one side of the so-called dichotomy within the other, to show that one is often a subset of the other, albeit sometimes a distorted subset—a subset that has forgotten its dependence upon the wider set." He believes that everything occurring is contained in "the more-than-human-world."

It is difficult for me to see how what he says can be anything but true. What I am calling the dominant worldview and the Indigenous worldview are both part of the more-than-human-world. Complementarity inherently flows through Nature. Recognizing it and then using it appropriately, however, is a challenge for humans. We can see our technological marvels as a part of Nature but we must also take into consideration the degree of harm technology can do to natural systems. Evidence shows that by ignoring certain laws of Nature, humans can create tremendous and unnecessary damage. For example, if one's worldview is that humans are at the top of creation, choices are significantly different and can upset the balance of Nature if implemented widely. Whether or not such a belief is a "subset" of a more rational truth, it is just as destructive as spending all day on a couch smoking cigarettes. In other words, without a conscious awareness of the original understanding of the five aspects this book presents, the behavior continues. The outcomes of the two worldviews are real and our choices have serious consequences. If I can show that one works better than the other in the five areas I have selected, let someone else write a book about the magic of Western technology and how it can partner with Indigenous science to improve both forms of magic. Thus, I see David's work and mine as different but complementary.[18] Although symbiotic potentialities can be discovered in both worldviews, common sense allows for "right or wrong" choices in life. When we move camps, we must decide what to leave behind. I am pointing out five crucial perceptions of the dominant worldview to leave behind, and offering proven options from Indigenous worldview to bring with us.

A Sense of Urgency

Last night, I sat with a number of retired Americans and Canadians here in the small Mexican fishing village near where I live. At one point in our wide-ranging conversations, someone asked me about my work with a local fishing community to create the first marine park on our Pacific Coast. While discussing predictions that by 2048, our world's oceans would have no more sustainable fisheries (Worm et al.), I asked if they had heard about our being in the middle of a likely "sixth mass extinction." In addition to not knowing about (or believing) the research on fish depletion, none of them had heard about the mass extinction warnings, and they were not interested in my description of it. Becoming aware of our impending challenges may be a prerequisite for thoroughly understanding the potentially transformative ideas in this book.[19]

A mass extinction, opposed to normal background extinction, occurs when a large percentage of life disappears in a relatively short time. According to one study, in the last century alone, the average rate of vertebrate species loss is more than 100 times greater than the normal rate (Cebellos et al.). "Extinction data revealed a rate of 100 to 1,000 species lost per million per year, mostly due to human-caused habitat destruction and climate change," according to Christine Dell'Amore's article in *National Geographic*. Most mass extinction researchers end their alarming warnings with more hopeful claims about being able to avoid or minimize this tragedy if we intensify our efforts to stop over-exploitation. Unfortunately, "intensified efforts" are now unlikely to be effective because even the most astute policymakers continue to use the same misguided assumptions about the world that brought us to this precipice. The recent United Nations climate talks (COP 21) in Paris support this concern. James Hansen, the first scientist to publicly warn about the danger of human-caused climate change, referred to the talks as "worthless words" (Milman).

Waking up to some of the realities facing us does not require focusing on the negative, becoming fearful, or getting angry. Keeping our heads out of the sand allows us to see all things, including the surrounding magic and beauty—even when we are living in the worst environments. Seeing, feeling, and thinking about destruction and the potential to avoid it can help us understand what Robin Kimmerer refers to in her beautiful book, *Braiding Sweetgrass*, as "the dual powers of destruction and creation that shape the world" (256). She is referring to how plants separate into strands that are rewoven into a new whole. She carefully describes the reciprocity involved in this process; without it, destruction continues. I contend that reflecting on the two major worldviews is a largely untapped way for us to come to understand the forces of destruction and regeneration. Life is a precious gift; we can choose to recognize illness, and work towards healing it, or not. This book is for those who want to do the work.

Chapter Overview

I have organized the chapters as the center along with four cardinal directions of a sacred Medicine Wheel. Each chapter describes an Indigenous worldview that contrasts with the dominant worldview.[20] Theory is combined with recommendations for learning and praxis, and exercises are suggested for actualizing personal and, ultimately, global transformation. "Explanatory notes" at the end of each chapter offer clarifications, enhancements, examples, support, or additional references. An appendix offers two ways I have personally used this Medicine Wheel's five components in an effort to heal myself and the world. I suggest that the reader can choose between reading this book backwards starting with the Appendix; or by reading all the explanatory notes first; or by starting at any of the middle chapters and bouncing around in the book. As with any Medicine Wheel, you can only start with where you are in your heart and any point on the wheel can bring you to higher and higher levels of insight.

(Citations are provided in MLA format rather than APA for an important reason explained in an endnote.)[21]

Chapter One: Trance-Based Learning

Chapter One represents the center of the Medicine Wheel, and describes how Indigenous worldview and cultural practices relate to understanding the power of trance-based learning or hypnotic states of concentration. This center, like the earth and sky that are often the center of Lakota Medicine Wheels, influences the four winds or directions interactively. Indigenous worldview assumes that alternative consciousness and what we refer to as "hypnotic phenomenon" can and must be used to create balance in the world. Indigenous people still use ceremony, vision quests, purification rituals, fasting, drumming, meditations, chanting, and other modalities to modify brain frequency and create higher levels of receptivity to learning. Without incorporating this into our natural way of being in the world, we are susceptible to being controlled by others, especially in a hierarchical society supported by the dominant worldview. With Indigenous understandings of the four dynamic forces represented in our Medicine Wheel, we can better access the deep wisdom of our unconscious. We can enhance our intuitive skills and communicate with all levels of consciousness and co-consciousness via the power of trance-based learning.

Chapter Two: Courage and Fearlessness

Next, we move toward the West, with its mysteriousness and magic representing the spirits. With generosity at the heart of this direction, we learn how best to move toward the sunset of our journey on Earth. Generosity is a core value in the majority of Indigenous cultures, often considered the highest expression of courage. In dominant worldview cultures, courage is theoretically honored, but feared as a mainstay of life. People avoid it in ultimately destructive ways. The goal of this chapter is to teach readers how to face the future with courage and trust the universe with fearlessness when action is taken. Using Indigenous worldview to overcome fear and its impact on creating and sustaining our problems will enable us to change the destructive socio-political system. Using stories and metacognitive strategies, I describe how to return to the courage and fearlessness of our ancestors and contemporaries.

Chapter Three: Self-Authorship

Moving clockwise to the North, this chapter addresses the spirits that nurture us during difficult times. It helps to guide us toward using our highest self when making choices. It recognizes that dominant culture tends to promote hierarchy. In traditional Indigenous belief systems, honest reflection about one's lived experience represents the highest authority for making life choices when one also understands that everything is interconnected. Interacting with fear and trance, perceptions of authority are crucial for understanding our global crises. I show how self-authorization can again work for everyone in conjunction with courage, fearlessness, and trance.

Chapter Four: Sacred Communication

The East is the direction of new beginnings. Here we focus on the importance of language and what we call the arts. Among Indigenous people, these are sacred vibrations to be used with great respect. The dominant worldview encourages deceptive communication on many levels. Lying and fraud are commonplace, often seen as necessary tools for social and economic relationships. Especially when used with spontaneous or induced trance awareness, words have the power to direct our beliefs and actions. This can be most unfortunate when deceptive intentions prevail. When carefully used to express the multi-faceted idea of "truth," expressive communications can also be healing. In this chapter, I explain how we can modify our Indo-European languages developed in alignment with the dominant worldview in order to better employ Indigenous worldview perspectives.

Chapter Five: Nature as All

The final chapter stands before the winds of the South where the sun is highest, and life is drawn from it to make things grow. Here we learn again how to see Nature as the ultimate model of truth, the ultimate teacher helping us live to our highest potential. As long as the dominant worldview remains anthropocentric, placing humans in a superior position, we have little chance of turning things around. This chapter helps us comprehend Nature in all its forms as our guide to the future, even for those of us living in urban centers. It shows how we can learn from Nature in ways that can save us from the pitfalls of hegemonic education.

This chapter ends with one of the most important lessons from Nature: complementarity. Although most of this book has polarized the Indigenous and dominant worldviews, when courage, self-authorship, use of words and art, and engagement with Nature are working according to Indigenous worldview, complementarity becomes a vital goal. This chapter reveals how seeking complementarity between all apparent opposites is essential for authentic world harmony.

Concluding Thoughts for This Introduction

In his popular book, *Dispelling Wetiko: Breaking the Curse of Evil*, Paul Levy refers to a Cree mythological monster, "Wetiko," or "Windigo" in similar

Anishinaabe stories. He explains that the stories about the monster were used to encourage moderation, self-control, and cooperation (31). Although we generally share the same concern, Levy's approach to addressing our crisis differs from mine, in that he fails to address our crisis as a worldview issue. He calls the problem a "virus" and a "malignant egophrenia" (31) that is "impossible to grasp with our cognitive, rational, conceptual mind" (32). Referring to the virus as an "instrument for the anti-Christ, i.e., evil," he states that this insanity may be a necessary way for us to experience the self-knowing that will ultimately bring us to the "salvation, redemption and incarnation of the Divine" (45). He only mentions worldview when he says the English language reflects it (22), an idea with which I agree and discuss in Chapter Three. Moreover, Levy offers no indication that there is anything in Indigenous wisdom or worldview that can mitigate the problems we now face caused by our collective behavior. He seems to assume that Indigenous cultures suffered similarly; why else would they have created stories about such monsters?

According to Levy, the solution is for all of us to rise to a higher level of consciousness, yet he admits that his own writing will likely spread the evil disease "if people reading the book don't have a more refined, rarefied, nuanced and sophisticated way of understanding what is being pointed at" (33). I believe that such understanding does require the "cognitive, rational and conceptual thinking" he says cannot help. In addition, we must realize the role of trance-based learning, as the next chapter describes in detail.

I prefer the solutions offered by Kimmerer in her Anishinaabe cultural interpretations about the monster. She writes that Windigos are not born from some evil force, but are somehow a divine intervention for transcendence, created when humans are out of balance and lose their sense of respect and reciprocity for all. In other words, prior to European contact, Indigenous peoples may have known the risks of departing from the original worldview. The ancient stories helped to create cultures that held on to the balance because of what they taught. The solution for Kimmerer is a worldview that does not see the world in terms of scarcity, but in terms of abundance and gratitude. "Scarcity and plenty are as much qualities of the mind and spirit as they are of the economy," she states (376). This worldview emphasizes the commons over private property, especially relating to local landscapes, and sharing rather than gluttony. Such a worldview offers a different orientation to concepts of fear, authority, words, and Nature, emphasizing abiding by the laws of Nature, as Daniel Wildcat reminds us in *Red Alert! Saving the Planet with Indigenous Knowledge.*

> The presumptuous-sounding claim that the Earth can be saved through indigenous knowledges at first seems more than a little arrogant: it sounds,

quite frankly, unindigenous. The idea of "saving the planet" with any knowledge, as understood in the context of the dominant Western worldview, will
connote the idea that we humans are in control of the Earth. However, such
an idea is foreign to (the Indigenous worldview) . . . To be honest we, human-
kind alone, cannot make such a claim. We will have to call on the help of our
relatives. We must pay attention and look to the plants, the animals, the wind,
the water, the Earth, and our most distant relative, the sun, to stop imminent
Earth catastrophe. It is precisely this help, from these, our other-than-human
relatives, that indigenous thinkers are not embarrassed to call on. (136)

An article by its researchers describes their proposed curriculum in the
peer-reviewed *New Horizons for Learning Journal* published by John Hopkins
University School of Education:

Worldviews profoundly impact individual and shared goals and desires,
shaping perceptions, motivations and values both consciously and unconsciously. Worldviews inform human behavior in relationships and choreo-
graph individual and social reactions and actions every moment of the day.
They shape our habits of introspection, analysis and communication, influ-
encing the questions we ask, how we make meaning of our experiences, and
ultimately the ways we learn. (Schlitz et al.)

It is past time for discussing the importance of worldviews, and critical to
begin the important work of investigating and reshaping them before it is too
late. This is what we can do together on the following pages; as Dan Moonhawk Alford writes: "Bringing these worldview issues to the forefront of consciousness, rather than having them influence us only subconsciously, is one
way to add new perspectives to some of our most vexing cultural problems."

Notes

1. Laurens van der Post offers this recollection of his good friend's original
   words. See http://www.ratical.org/many_worlds/LvdP/quotations.html
2. Noam writes this in his published endorsement of the book *Teaching Truly: A
   Curriculum to Indigenize Mainstream education.*
3. Some people in non-Indian cultures still harbor their Indigenous worldview to
   some degree, and some in Native cultures know they have been indoctrinated
   into the dominant worldview. What is important is to be conscious of both, and
   then make appropriate choices about how to resonate with the highest truths.
4. There were three according to Redfield, but by the 1900s, the Orient began
   to imitate the West. The idea of these two worldviews makes sense when one
   studies the many worldview essays other than those relating to "the Christian
   worldview" that compare and contrast "Indigenous" and "Western" paradigms.
5. My own initial sensibilities relating to such a comparison came to me not via
   scholarly research but from a vision that I experienced shortly after a "near-

death experience" while attempting to kayak the Rio Urique in Mexico. Although I have written about what emerged as a theory in *Primal Awareness: A True Story . . .* in 1998, this book represents my effort to truly help others make operational the idea that our original worldview can save us from ourselves. I retell the story in the last chapter about learning from the animals since my vision came from a dear and a mountain lion.

6. Riane Eisler in *The Chalice and the Blade* writes that humans moved from a partnership model to a dominator model around 7,000 years ago. Some say it started at the dawn of agriculture; however, in my view, when agriculture led to considerable surplus, the real problems began a bit later. In a chapter on "A Positive View of Human Nature and its Potential" in a highly respected work on the history of peace, Sponsel offers a similar timeline: "Palaeo-anthropological evidence and interpretations indicate that the human line evolved at least by 4 million years ago, agriculture about 10,000 years ago, and the state around 5,000 years ago" (105).

7. I use "entranced" to suggest that some degree of what we describe as hypnotic phenomenon or trance-based learning may be involved in this historical transformation, whereby people relinquished control of their potential for hypnosis to authoritarian outsiders.

8. For a more comprehensive treatment of anti-Indianism, see my edited volume from the University of Texas, *Unlearning the Language of Conquest: Scholars Expose Anti-Indianism in America.*

9. Socrates: *"I'm a lover of learning, and trees and open country won't teach me anything, whereas men in the city do."* Plato, *Phaedrus*, 230d.

10. Darwin's fellow countryman, English explorer William Parker Snow, visited the same Indigenous tribal people of Tierra del Fuego in 1855, and without Darwin's racist and evolutionary presuppositions, came to very different conclusions about each of Darwin's uninformed claims about the Fuegians (262).

11. For an excellent comparison between Indigenous and dominant worldview-based levels of social and personal happiness, see the chapter "Happiness and Indigenous Wisdom in the History of the Americas" by Frank Bracho, in *Unlearning the Language of Conquest* (29–45) University of Texas Press.

12. The best knowledge and wisdom combined will yield our guide to survival. This includes primary source evidence from: the logs of conquerors and pioneers who "discovered" Indigenous people; honest missionaries and soldiers who "changed sides" upon admiring the joy, health, and freedom of people they encountered; relatively unbiased anthropology and archeology; and careful, open-minded observations of traditional Indigenous cultures.

13. See Luke Barnesmoore's article on how the CIA constructed this phrase in order to silence alternative thinking. "Conspiracy Theory as Symbolic Epistemic Mechanism and Non-human Actor."

14. A friend once reminded me of how bad things are among Indigenous nations today in terms of domestic violence, drug addiction, and corruption, saying it was evidence that whatever the worldview, they had caused the same problems as we are all facing under the dominant worldview. My response was to distinguish between genocide and suicide.

There is no doubt we are now all "in the same boat."

15. Fabro's seminal studies published in the *Journal of Peace Research* explain that dependence on "the state" requires the self-destructive violence that surrounds us including: "internal and external conflict; threats from external enemies; social stratification and other forms of structural inequality and violence; centralized authority; and police and military organization" (68) [FN]. Lewellen's text, *Evolution of the State*, essentially agrees. Thwarting beliefs that help maintain state violence requires that we educate ourselves to counter the hegemonic baseline assumptions we employ ecologically, philosophically, spiritually, psychologically, and socially.

16. To understand how Indigenous people, especially women, are encountering neoliberalism, see *Indigenous Encounters with Neoliberalism* by Isabel Altamirano-Jimenez.

17. For scholar support of this argument, see Schmidt, Ryan W. "American Indian Identity and Blood Quantum in the 21st Century: A Critical Review." *Journal of Anthropology*. 2011. Web.

18. Another acquaintance and pen pal, Daniel Pinchbeck, believes that the problems on earth today are simply a rite of passage to a better place. I have told him I think what we are doing might have this potential, but to call it so now fails to recognize the requirements of the Indigenous rite of passage.

19. I believe we have to be brutally honest about what we are up against but at the same time never lose sight of the beauty, magic, and wonderful gifts that surround us. Then we can commit to reflection and transformation.

20. Although there are common beliefs in each worldview, some of the differences are literally killing us.

21. The academic-oriented reader or one familiar with the publisher's usual use of APA (American Psychological Association) style may notice that this is not the style I use for citations. In keeping with Indigenous research approaches that are decolonizing and aware of neoliberal and unethical systems, I have abandoned my 30-year use of APA citations in protest of its support for the CIA's illegal torture policies. In mid-December 2014, I wrote an article for *Truthout* entitled, "Are Eugenics, Torture and Social Control Hidden Legacies of the American Psychological Association?" In July 2015, a 542-page Independent report commissioned by the APA Board of Directors confirmed my allegations about the APA's significant collusion and cover up of the tragic illegal interrogations used by the U.S. government. APA is the nation's largest scientific and psychological association. It proved its powerful influence in the world with its horrific historical and recent engagements. This may be the first book written with this symbolic protest in mind.

1

Trance-Based Learning (TBL)

*Traditional Indigenous societies did not separate "ordinary reality"
from "non-ordinary reality" as we do today. The trance state was socially
acknowledged and accepted as a method of balancing body, mind, and soul
and of bringing back into harmony that which had caused dissonance.*

—Nana Nauwald

*You use hypnosis not as a cure but as a means of establishing
a favorable climate in which to learn.*

—Milton H. Erickson

In 1997 don Miguel Ruiz published a little book entitled *The Four Agreements.* Considered to be in the "New Age" genre, it has sold over 5 million
copies, has been on the New York Times best-sellers list for over eight years,
and has been translated into 38 languages. Biographies of Ruiz explain that
after becoming a physician, a near-death experience brought him back to
the healing traditions of his traditional Indigenous heritage—including a
mother who was a healer and a grandfather who was a shaman.[1] While writing about four positive agreements that can help end a person's many negative agreements[2] he refers to two concepts repeatedly. The first is "words,"

the focus of our Medicine Wheel's third direction (Chapter 4). I counted 41 specific references to "word" or "words" in his book and many more referring to ideas about what people say or think. Here are a few examples:

The word is so powerful that one word can change a life... (27).

One word is like a spell, and humans use the word like black magicians... (28).

The word can enter our mind and change our whole belief for better or ... (29).

Misuse of our word is putting us deeper and deeper into hell (41).

Breaking agreements is very difficult because we put the power of the word (115).

The second concept he mentioned very often is "imagination":

"Just imagine what you can create..."(44).

"Just imagine the day you stop..." (76).

"Imagine that you have the ability to see the world with different eyes" (129).

"Imagine that you have permission to be happy..."(130).

"Imagine living your life without judging others" (132).

I begin this chapter by pointing all of this out to the reader because what is behind the truth and importance of his references to words and imagination is never mentioned. Without understanding this and other Indigenous worldview implications that relate to the five chapters of *Point of Departure*, I do not believe acknowledging the wisdom of the four agreements can lead to personal or global transformation. First of all, without understanding that the reason words have such power is because of TBL[3] and the phenomenon of hypnosis, imagining alone is seldom transformational. Secondly, without understanding the nature of TBL, the words are unlikely to have an effect. For example, "Imagining you have permission to be happy" even if it were seeded during trance state receptivity, would only literally create a sense of permission while a person continued being unhappy. Similarly, "having the ability to see the world with different eyes" would only implant the suggestion giving ability without changing the psychological programming one is trying to modify.

Such subtle but vital differences are explained below. My point here is that without understanding naturalistic trance phenomenon as our ancestors did for thousands of years, it is difficult to take the beautiful truisms that resonate through Ruiz's wonderful book and implement them with cognitive will and determination. In other words, to implement Ruiz's four important commitments to being honest, not taking things personally, not making assumptions and doing one's best, there are requirements we address in this book that include Indigenous worldview perspectives that go deeper:

1. Using trance to assure images actually change beliefs and brain wiring. (Chapter 1)
2. Changing dominant culture's aversion to fear and learning to use it to practice a virtue and to turn courage into fearlessness. (Chapter 2)
3. Setting aside all sources of authority for beliefs and choices and using only honest reflection on lived experience in concert with one's highest self and oneness with all. (Chapter 3)
4. Knowing the pitfalls of the English language and why words are as powerful as Ruiz clearly says they are and using other forms of communication to help stay on course. (Chapter 4)
5. Referring to the other-than-human and more-than-human natural world as law and teacher. (Chapter 5).

Although Ruiz does not teach about TBL, his words on the back cover of his book show that he understands that this combination of words and imagination is really about trance-based learning when he presents a prayer.[4] He starts his prayer with a classic example of hypnotic script: "Close your eyes ... Focus your attention on your lungs, as if only you lungs exist. Feel the pleasure when your lungs expand. . . . Take a deep breath and feel the air as it fills your lungs. Feel how the air is nothing but love" (Ruiz 139). However, the hypnosis is unlikely to happen when reading a book and because there is no mention of TBL, it is less likely to engage the other worlds and dimensions also mentioned in his book.

It seems that Ruiz understands how easy it is for people to be swayed by words even though he does not risk the negative feedback he might have gotten by referring to it as "hypnosis." Unlike Ruiz, Levy's book (mentioned at the end of the previous chapter) does refer to modern people as those who have become "hypnotized and entranced by their own inflated self-image" (Lecy 314). I do not know if he intended to refer to actual hypnosis or not, as he says nothing more about the idea. In any case, I do agree that spontaneous mass hypnosis and negative trance-based learning[5] can lead us down the wrong road but only if we are unaware of the power of words when we are in a natural brain-wave frequency that makes us hyper suggestible to words and images. Once we are aware and take control of this natural phenomenon then not only can we avoid accidental or externally authorized hypnotic images, but the power of hypnosis and trance-based learning becomes a tool we can use any time.

Personal beliefs, including many created during early childhood traumas, play a huge role in both personal and collective assumptions about the world, as well as in subsequent behaviors. Of course anyone can fall into negative behaviors regardless of their worldview. How a given culture or society attempts to prevent such behaviors (on individual and community levels) is part of the great and essential diversity of humanity; and a fundamental worldview can be responsible for guiding these different cultural efforts. The practical use of trance was an important reality for our ancestors before the point of departure, and it remains an integral part of life for pockets of Indigenous people who still recognize its power. Trance has helped people to access feelings, ideas, beliefs, information, and creative insights in ways not normally accessed in waking consciousness. Trance-based learning was—throughout the ages prior to our point of departure—part of the equation that led communities to "walk the talk" of such virtues as generosity, courage, patience, respectfulness, honesty, fortitude, and humility.

From my time with the Raramuri Simerone people living in caves deep in the Copper Canyon area of Mexico, I learned that the four major influences on trance related to certain understandings about four concepts: Fear, Authority, Words, and Nature (the topics of the remaining chapters in this book). In the Indigenous worldview, fear offers an opportunity to practice a virtue; authority comes only from honest reflection on lived experience with the realization that everything is related; words and other forms of communication are understood as sacred vibrations, and nature was the ultimate teacher. Before the reader uses the techniques for TBL I present here, it is important that you carefully read rest of the book. For now, it may be helpful to remember this is all about what I call the CAT-FAWN connection. CAT stands for "Concentration-Activated Transformation" which refers to TBL. And FAWN represents the four forces mentioned above. What is most important is that dominant worldview assumptions about these four concepts (Fear, Authority, Words, and Nature) are dangerously different than those stemming from the Indigenous Worldview.

Although I refer to terms like Concentration-Activated Transformation," "trance-based learning," "hypnosis or self-hypnosis" traditional Indigenous communities did not have such terms but merely recognized such mental functions as part of natural phenomenon. According to traditional Indigenous healers around the world, there is a vital energy within us and in the world, the source of which is creation itself. In Indigenous ceremonies, the energy of the land, plants, animals, fish, insects, plants, rocks and rivers are respected and evoked. In Indigenous worldview trance relates to this energy. They understand the phenomenon as a holistic, naturalistic shift of energy that allows for subtle but profound changes, which in turn open up extraordinary powers within us.

Indeed, a number of spiritual traditions that are practiced today have emerged from this ancient realization (Sorenson) (Some of these traditions move practitioners into the Indigenous worldview, but more often contemporary practices are only diversions from the Indigenous ways). For example, Kundalini is an energy thought to circulate through the body. People used ancient medicine wheels that helped tribal peoples focus on cycles of life energy as Kundalini practitioners uses chakras (Sanskrit for circle, wheel, or cycle). Chi or ki, which martial artists have used since ancient times to tap into to achieve amazing feats of strength and agility, is an energy that stems from trance work. Prana, spirit and soul reference numerous ways of applying traditional, very old realizations about energy exchanges. For all of the options, changing from normal consciousness with the intent to gain better access to living in harmony is about connecting to and rebalancing subtle energies that surround and fill us. Trance-based learning is, in its various forms, how we bring such energies to a level of consciousness.

Referring to the use of trance to communicate with visible and invisible energies, the late David Maybury-Lewis, Director of the "Millennium" television series, anthropology professor emeritus at Harvard, and author of *Millennium: Tribal Wisdom and the Modern World*, writes: "We can no longer assume that our modern way of life represents the most advanced stage of progress (210)." He talks about the relationship between humans and spirits as one of mutual responsibility. Of the many tribes he intensely studied, he noted that for most of them contact between people and the spirit world permeates every aspect of their lives. Even the tribe Maybury-Lewis thought might be an exception still saw it as vital.

> We had been wrong about the Xavante. We thought they were an eminently social people, more interested in politics than in cosmology. Yet the apparently practical Xavante allow for—no insist on—ceremonial pauses during which they danced themselves into states of trance to commune with the spiritual forces of their universe. (ibid)

Such communication between worlds is mediated with trance. Trance-based learning as a reciprocal communication with "others" to whom we are connected is different from the individually focused therapeutic use of trance and its many cousins such as biofeedback, hypnosis, placebo, or mind training. The idea that trance-based learning has something to do with communicating with co-conscious[6] entities sounds more superstitious than scientific. However, even neuroscience has identified such complementary forces at work in our universe. Trance-based learning seems to relate to changes in brainwaves, with lower frequency vibrations generally allowing for deeper learning (alpha and theta rather than beta).[7] However, the process is likely much more complicated, even beyond the reach of neuroscience. For example of the complexity, a rigorous study conducted by a group of scientists at the University of Szeged in Hungary found that hypnosis substantially enhanced learning by essentially diminishing competition within our brains between fundamentally incompatible modes of learning (Nemeth et al 801). One mode has to do with how we categorize things and another about how we remember procedural processes.[8] Other brain scientists have referred to the "complementary" aspect of these apparently opposing learning functions of the brain (Aizenstein).[9]

Another expression of such complementary communication resulting from trance-based learning relates to the belief in co-conscious communication outside one's self, a belief that is firmly entrenched in Indigenous worldview as noted above. Such co-conscious communication might have played a role in how the Lakota and other plains tribes of the Americas who captured feral Spanish horses became such masterful equestrians so quickly. The tribesmen employed their understanding that, via trance (a phenomenon both humans and horses can access), they could communicate with the horses.[10] Western science has studied "animal hypnosis," but most studies, far from holistic observations, generally conclude that animals enter trance only for "tonic immobility" to protect themselves against predators. My own experience confirms the Indigenous understanding and reveals something more similar to human trance-based learning. The following anecdote is one of many that led me independently to this conclusion.

While I was an adjunct professor in the Department of Psychology at UC Berkeley, I was teaching hypnosis certification for Marriage, Family, and Child Counseling and serving as Vice President of the Northern California Society of Clinical Hypnosis, while at the same time I was also working with wild mustangs adopted from the Bureau of Land Management. At first, I saw no connection between the hypnosis work and the horse training. I was involved in competitive endurance riding and wanted to use wild horses instead of the standard breed for the sport, the Arabian. I had no experience in horse training "unbroken" horses. It did not, however, take long for me to realize that the newly captured creatures reacted as if in hypnotic trance.

When I tried to approach the first mustang I brought home, I was unable to get close enough to touch him without his kicking at me. Each time I came close, his body would tense and the white around his brown pupils expanded. Eventually, I tried a new approach, one that came to me in a vision actually.[11] Instead of my "cowboy" use of ropes and aggression, I attempted to talk with him using some other faculty of mind. Ideas like "telepathy" combined with "empathy" come closest to describing the feeling for me. The next time I approached him, he did not immediately opt for his fight-or-flight reaction. He seemed to be listening and considering the option to cooperate with me. Unlike the animals in tonic immobility, he and the many wild horses I subsequently "trained," were highly attentive to every move I made. They were automatically exercising a fourth survival mechanism perhaps. Not fight, flight or freezing, but a hyper receptivity to a perceived trusted other. It was as if they were accepting the possibility that they could trust in my authority.

After a couple of years of success with a dozen or more adopted mustangs, some that I adopted and others that had been abandoned in fields because they could not be caught, I got to where I could put a beginning rider on a horse which had been captive less than a week. A television program called "Evening Magazine" contacted me to do a segment about my work. For it we brought in a wild mustang that had recently been captured. After tying the frightened horse between two posts about ten feet apart, I explained to the show's host, Richard Hart, what I planned on doing. When the cameras started rolling, the horse violently reared in an effort to escape, and after falling down stood aggressively waiting. My goal was to approach him and get on his back.[12]

Putting myself into a light trance and using what I can only describe as a sort of intuitively derived telepathic skill, I looked at the four-year old mustang indirectly, towards the ground, and began my approach. I starting singing, intuitively feeling the sound would help us both stay calm and confident. I stepped carefully with a sideways shuffle toward the horse, stopping alongside his left leg so he could not easily kick me. Then I turned so I was facing the same direction as he was. I slowly raised my hand under his neck so I could stroke the opposite side of his head. He reacted with a jerk, pulling his head up higher than I could reach. The white in his eye grew bigger. I deepened my own trance state, took a breath and released it, then I "told" him it was going to be OK. I told him to trust me. I say I "told him," but in reality my thoughts were conveyed telepathically. I wanted him to know that if he did any more rearing and kicking he was going to hurt himself.

Soon his head started to lower and the white of his eyes started to show less and less. When his head was almost resting on my shoulder with our eyes at the same level, I brought my arm back and stepped back behind his shoulders once again, he reacted. His large head immediately raised and the white returned. I touched him gently on the back, resumed the patter of my language and song that was more about helping me maintain what felt like a psychic groove or telepathic focus. I put more pressure on his back with both of my hands, increasing it as I carefully jumped up and down until I was high enough to swing my leg over and sit astride him. I knew when I vaulted upon his back as I intended, I would land where a mountain lion would land and the horse had instinctive reactions for this. It would have been the time he would have bucked and twisted violently, throwing me and perhaps stomping me. But he just stood there, not at all paralyzed with fear or in a state of hypnotic immobility, but paying close attention to me and whatever communicative energy I was managing to share. When I landed on his back, his ears immediately stretched back toward me, but he continued to trust the vibrations I was sending.

The horse's trance was not merely about freezing as a protection mechanism at all, but was a kind of intuitive realization of trust or an act of knowing that came from some place other than normal "thinking" or instinct (Jacobs). Both the horse and I employed an ability largely absent in cultures operating under the dominant worldview. We both fully realized that all learning comes from experience and that all experience happens in two worlds at the same time. Anything that keeps us from perceiving in both places prevents us from fully learning.

The story of the horse conveys this idea of trance work being natural and that we have access to ways of learning and communicating that can put us in touch with multiple dimensions of self as well as of other. In the Indigenous worldview, this has long been understood as "oneness" or "interconnectedness" with all of life. David Peat writes, "Indigenous coming to knowing means entering into relationship with the spirits of knowledge, with plants and animals, with beings that animate dreams and visions and with the spirit of the people" (Peat 65). Webb reveals in her study that the Natives told her the best way to learn, called *yanantin* or a way to live in complementarity with others, was to go into deep trance with mescaline from the juice of a cactus. "It was suggested to me at the beginning of my research that the best way for me to understand and integrate this concept of *yanantin* was for me to "download" it—that is, to go into ceremony with the San Pedro cactus" (Webb 78).

Plant medicines, like ayahuasca for example, do induce trance-based learning and themselves can be great teachers of oneness. However, results depend on how much understanding of Indigenous precepts a participant has. Roan Kaufman's dissertation supports this view, showing that long-time users who have studied Indigenous worldview precepts as part of their ayahuasca journey become more insightful and autonomous in the world than those who have had little experience with it. The current interest in ayahuasca would become more practical for individuals and the world when applying such wisdom and skills that relate to its use. Such knowledge and emphasis of virtues and behaviors relating to interconnectedness, courage, and generosity make a big difference in the value of experience, in contrast to experimental, recreational, or otherwise unprepared use of hallucinogenic substances. Cognitive pre-learning (beta learning), discipline, courage, and other appropriate preparations are essential. Becoming expert in the use of trance-based learning can give us access and control of ways of being that can help us bring social/ecological systems back to a flowing balance. Mike Williams of the University of Reading writes in his text, *Prehistoric Belief,* that early humans were adept at entering trances and used trance-state to solve a number of life-threatening problems that we still encounter today.

Plant medicines, however, are only one way traditional Indigenous societies utilized trance-based learning. A variety of cultural rituals, group or individual prayer ceremonies such as involved purification lodges, vision quests, and other forms of isolated meditation, intentional trance-inducing dance rituals (Thomason), drumming and other forms of music (Amoss, Doak), physical exertion followed by trance induction, fasting, and sensory deprivation (Villoldo & Krippner) were all widely practiced as ways to embed important knowledge into the psyche for healing (Walsh, Thomason). Considerations about cultural expectations as well as personal and community values and goals, were often presented during storytelling both preceding and following such trance-inducing experiences. The result was that people could enter into light trance any time without such dramatic work, whenever the need for a stronger, more fully optimal response to life's situation called for it.[13]

Such knowledge, however, has not yet re-seeded itself into our collective global worldview. Few people see plants as "nations" or "teachers," so using trance to communicate with them would not make sense. Hypnosis is a fringe phenomenon in itself for most people. A few microbiologists connect epigenetics and hypnosis phenomena to show how the fabric of our genetic identities is subject to environmental stimuli,[14] and a number of philosophers refer to "phenomenal unification" being the result of possibilities to simultaneously access "co-consciousness" outside of our own. However, the scientists truly pushing for the understanding on a level comparable to Indigenous worldview, like Rupert Sheldrake for example, have a difficult time making their way into the mainstream.

The Bible also contains references to the power of trance, such as Peter's trance that led to his empathy with the Gentiles. However, in spite of this (or because of it?), one mandate says that trance phenomenon is a form of witchery and is an abomination to God (Deuteronomy 18). Thus, interpretations of this passage have succeeded in stifling the use of trance-based learning or communication among Christians.[15] Of course, trance work is seldom seen in K–12 schooling, and in spite of its proven success in healing, most medical schools do not teach it (Askay et al). Even the placebo effect in medicine, which is a hypnosis or trance phenomenon, is being minimized today. For hundreds of years, physicians have witnessed the power of belief to cure but it is usually overshadowed with medical interventions. Most doctors know about placebo, but few want people to know about healings that do not require medical interventions. Two Harvard scholars, Herbert Benson and Ted Kaptchuk, have stood firmly against years of ridicule and dismissal of the facts that show that from 30 to 90 percent of successful results from the actual drugs or surgery occur with placebo comparisons, even when the patient knows he or she is in the placebo group. Benson's history of this unfortunate process up until 1995 can be found in his text, *Timeless Healing: The Power and Biology of Belief,* and his co-authored article in the *Journal of the American Medical Association* back in 1975 entitled, "The Placebo Effect – a Neglected Asset." Kaptchuk's 1998 journal article "Intentional Ignorance" purports that the medical profession may be worried people are going to catch on to the power of the body-mind. He writes about this in a 1994 *New England Journal of Medicine* article stating that placebo controls are unethical and have little to no efficacy in medical practice (Rothman & Michels 394–398).[16]

I have had experience in this anti-hypnosis controversy as well. Prentice-Hall's emergency medicine division, Brady, published my text, *Patient Communication for First Responders: The First Hour of Trauma,* in 1988. Field-tested for 12 years, it showed that first responders at the scene of an emergency, especially fire fighters, police, and paramedics, were using hypnosis whether they knew it or not, for good or for bad, because patients were in hypnotic states. "All creatures, during times of stress, become hyper-suggestible to the communication of perceived authority figures" (Jacobs 44). Thus, a paramedic or anyone else speaking with authority unintentionally could cause untold harm with an offbeat comment in front of an apparently unconscious person, like "Wow, that knee is messed up. I doubt he'll walk again." Or, with conscious effort based on simple training protocols, one could direct a patient to stop bleeding as in a situation where the victim is trapped in a car and direct pressure cannot be applied. After six months on the market and many letters from people around the world giving testimony to the life-saving techniques taught in the book, the book was taken off the market because, I was told, a lawyer or two determined the book should only be used by licensed medical physicians trained in medical hypnosis.

Thus, intentional use of trance-based learning is not a regular part of our daily lives and we have lost our ability and our inclination to intentionally use trance skills. Worse, we have inadvertently given control of the phenomenon to our preachers, peddlers and politicians – or any other person we allow to have significant authority over us. We have temporarily lost the wisdom that came from millions of years of observation in settings where we were not separated from the Natural world. We will never know to what degree trance employment brought our ancestors peace, sustainability and joy, in addition to millions of years of survival with clean water and air. There is however no doubt that trance became a core part of the worldview of otherwise very diverse Indigenous cultures. After the point of departure, however, we overshadowed our intuitive, arts-based, imaginal co-conscious with a more focused and ultimately imbalanced use of our rational mind alone. It is time, maybe past time, for us to re-embrace our trance-based learning skills and use.

Self-Hypnosis and Meditation

Self-hypnosis and meditation are generally practices that aim toward gaining some form of wisdom, whether for enlightenment or for stress management as is often the goal of meditation, or simply replacing a bad habit with a healthier option, a common objective of hypnosis. There are numerous ways to implement these fundamental concepts which are found in a variety of religious, spiritual, and healing traditions. Self-hypnosis and meditation are different from each other in that meditation involves being open to whatever comes, whereas hypnosis generally focuses on a specific outcome.

Many meditation strategies seek learning without explicit expectation. They intend to offer nondiscriminatory wisdom that is independent from reason and ego. Even though some meditative techniques repetitively chant words like "love" or "joy," the idea of no time and no space is more significant than the meaning of the word. A Zen master described this to me when I was in a Peace Bell ceremony at Hiroshima, Japan. The bell, designed in 1964, has etched into it a map of the world with no national boundaries. Where the log hits the bell to make the deep vibratory sound that blends with the surrounding participants' prayers for peace, there is a symbol for atomic energy. I was also told by a Zen master that at this point on the map, the longitude and latitude of the world is zero. This happens to be in the middle of the Atlantic Ocean. "Until we can be at zero, we cannot be one with all, and this is a requirement for peace," he told me.

When Japanese Zen masters practiced their meditations, it seems that they assumed an intimate relationship between humans and nature. I have not observed this, however, among many non-Indigenous meditators operating according to a more human-centered, dominant worldview. In any case, this relationship always exists in traditional Indigenous medita tion. Long ago I watched a Raramuri man who sat still and quietly all day on a cliff overlooking Mexico's Copper Canyon. Sitting cross legged right on the edge, his head tracked from the left to the right so slowly it took him ten minutes before he was looking to the right and started the movement back to the left. I was going in and out of camp throughout the day so he must have been there for eight hours. When he was done, he called me over and pointed to a number of things I never would have seen. He pointed at things several thousand feet below such as a drinking hole reflecting the last of the sun's rays and a deer grazing on a patch of some kind of vegetation. I asked my translator to ask him if he was looking for such things and he smiled telling me no. Nonetheless, the connection between the landscape and his concentration was clear, as was my realization that his people had been practicing such meditation for a long time. The idea of place-based knowledge is intrinsically woven into this approach.

Australian Aboriginals refer to *Dadirri* as Indigenous philosophy whereas Zen meditation is often considered anti-philosophy. A form of quietly aware watching and deep listening with "more than the ears... *Dadirri* is thought to be essential for guiding people toward respectful behavior" (Atkinson 15) with "all relations." Perhaps its philosophical side comes with "reflective non-judgmental consideration of what is being seen and heard and, having learnt from the listening, a purposeful plan to act, with actions informed by learning, wisdom, and the informed responsibility that comes with knowledge" (16).

In the Sun Dance ceremony (illegal in the United States from 1904 to 1978), I have stood watching the sun slowly rise above the horizon without blinking and seeing things in the sun that other dancers also saw. I danced for hours watching the leaves of a sacred dying tree until I saw healing images or ancestors or any number of visions that I reflected upon much later and that transformed my thinking. In addition to these meditations, I employed hypnosis when I hung from the tree by my piercing sticks or dragged the buffalo skulls. Using the pain to focus deeply, I imagined and verbally "prayed" (sending vibrations of intention into the universe and inviting communication with the spirits) for healing others. With the piercing I intentionally become one with the experience at the same time I imagine that peace can come to all, or that an uncle's last days will be joyful, or that a grandson's anger will be healed. Such "hypnosis" directs imaginings of a preconceived outcome, one that may have come from meditation, and remains the focus until belief in the image changes energies that can be internalized or transferred into the universe.

According to Western science, both meditation and hypnosis actually change the brain when practiced effectively. For example, when subjects are hypnotized to see a color other than the one shown to them, the place in the brain that scientists believe activates when the actual color is seen is what activates even when a different color is shown (Kosslyn et al). Research into "brain plasticity" demonstrates this as well. Whether from continual repetition as a source of learning, like learning to juggle, regular meditation practice or hypnotic visualization, when neurons are activated, a bond between them strengthens. There is a bilateral increase in the gray matter of the occipito-temporal cortex that can happen in a relatively short time (Draganski et al. and Luders et al.).[17] Of course, such detached, objective descriptions like these are far from the metaphorical explanations of Indigenous science and do little to help us contextualize the realities in ways that help us live in harmony with all.

Greg Cajete, in our book *Critical Neurophilosophy and Indigenous Wisdom*, explains this idea of metaphorical science further:

> Unless one is open to metaphoric thinking, Indigenous natural philosophy will remain mysterious because it has evolved from multi-level and multi-layered symbols that came to us long ago when we could talk to the animals and hear the gods or God more easily perhaps. Perhaps the shaman was the ultimate hypnotherapist, but hypnosis was always oriented toward the healing of relationships. Illness was often thought to be caused by improper relationship to the natural world, to the spiritual world, to the community and/or to one's own spirits. (116)

Nonetheless, I continue to use references to Western science, both to respect its potential complementarity and so the average reader will have a more familiar orientation, in order to establish the credibility of trance-based learning. Thomas Budzynski, an American psychologist and a pioneer in the field of electromyographic biofeedback in the 1960s, spoke of these connections between ancient Indigenous and modern approaches to hypnosis.

> Twenty-thousand years ago shamans used a variety of procedures to prepare their "clients" for the magical words and incantations that would remove evil spirits that affected the mind, body and spirit. Almost every one of these healing techniques could be said to comprised of two factors: (1) The preparation, which involved the production of what we might now call an altered state of consciousness and (2) The delivery or presentation of the healing or "change message . . . Most modern scientists would agree that the majority of these primitive healing procedures were just placebo ceremonies enhanced by the preparatory exercises that often produced an altered state. But then

the question might be asked, why does an altered state enhance the power of the magical words?

How to Employ Trance-Based Learning (TBL)

There are many ways to employ TBL. They include practicing various forms of meditation; tuning into other-than-human life (or what David Abram calls "more-than-human" ones), participating in song and art, practicing telepathy, hallucinogenic substances, and crying for a vision. Each can be used to learn a way of being or to help move your energies, feelings, and behaviors into different or expanded areas. Many approaches can only be created by you. Others involve strict protocols from trusted practitioners. For this chapter I focus on using self-hypnotic suggestions for finding and implementing intentional goals that spring from the Indigenous understandings of the topics of the next four chapters. The self-hypnosis will help readers take the conclusions from their metacognitive work within our Medicine Wheel and implement them in the real world. I briefly divide the steps into Induction and Directives (or Suggestions)

Inductions

Budzynski endorsed an easy approach developed in the psychophysiology lab at the Menninger Clinic Psychiatric Hospital that I have used in clinical and sports hypnosis practice effectively. The protocol is called "The Menninger 6-Step Process for Programming" and describes a six-step process for projecting visual images into the unconscious. They include:

1. Move first into a state of quietness and peripheral warmth and comfort.
2. While in this state, construct the visualization to be planted in the unconscious, a visualization that has already been carefully planned by the cortex, with ambiguities eliminated (for the unconscious is like a computer in some ways, and tends to take instructions literally).
3. Allow awareness to sink down into the theta state[18] with the idea that the unconscious is now listening; it is now in "record mode."
4. Gently project the visualization into the "field of mind" as a Gestalt, with as little left-cortex activity as possible.
5. Terminate the session with a quiet command, such as "do it," "so be it," or "the instruction is now terminated," in order to terminate unconscious receptivity (similar to using the "enter" key in programming a computer).

6. Bring awareness back to the surroundings carefully so as not to disturb the planted instruction (Green & Green 122).

Give it a try. Start by putting yourself in a comfortable position. It does not matter whether you are lying down or sitting up as long as you are comfortable. Your eyes should be closed and relaxation is enhanced when you take two or three deep breaths. You merely need to think the following suggestions, without saying anything aloud. Your first suggestion is, "Now I am going into the hypnotic state of consciousness." Slowly repeat this in your mind three times, and you will begin to slip into hypnosis. To achieve a slightly greater depth, simply say to yourself, "I am going deeper, and am more and more relaxed." You may want to imagine yourself going down an escalator or walking down stairs or a hill while you count backward from ten to zero, seeing yourself step down with each count. Picture yourself stepping off at the bottom when you reach zero, ready to receive your pre-determined instructions. Then begin imagining as much as you can about these instructions or goals becoming a reality of your own making. Believe with all your heart in the image that you are actualizing the new way of thinking, feeling, being, or acting.

The Eye Roll is another induction that can be used effectively for self-hypnosis. This involves looking as high as possible with the eyes while at the same time taking a deep breath and closing the eyelids. After a moment, allow the eyes to lower while exhaling and visualizing a falling leaf. When the leaf finally falls to the ground, assume that you are in sufficient hypnosis to receive suggestions. If not do this three or four times until you feel you are "imagining" your goals in a relatively deep manner. The more you can bring images of natural landscape you're your pictures the more powerful they will be. Connect to a particular location that you can remember that made you feel good. The energy from this place will assist you and the spirits from there can help create your more truthful and helpful trans-formations. Carl Jung's therapeutic technique of active imagination may be seen as a "gentle form of vision quest" (Jung 44), without the isolation, deprivation, and pain.

> In the process of active imagination the mind is stilled, and eventually a spontaneous mental image is allowed to enter awareness. The image is focused on and allowed to play itself out. Afterward, a record such as a drawing or a narrative is made, and finally what is learned from the experience is incorporated into everyday life (Jung 45). (in Thomason)

These and many other self-hypnotic techniques can be gleaned from a variety of Internet sources. What is most important for our goals is to use suggestions that stem from worldview reflection with specific references to the goals of the following chapter relating to:

- How to know your fears fully and honestly and how become courageous and let fear be a catalyst for practicing a virtue. Such as generosity, patience, fortitude, or courage.
- Use honest reflection on your own lived experience as your highest source of authority for what you know is the highest road to walk
- Be extremely aware of the power of language and choose words carefully
- Incorporate the natural world and its energies in your trance work whenever possible. If you cannot go into nature, bring it to you in the form of a feather or sage, etc.

Another set of induction techniques has to do with ideomotor neuron activation (Makuuchi et al). This is a phenomenon whereby when you imagine doing a small physical activity like having your finger move and you imagine it sufficiently strongly the neurons in the muscle groups that would normally do the movement stimulate the movement seemingly automatically without the actual movement of the finger. Using ideomotor activation can bring you into trance and at the same time let you know for sure you are in a state of hypnotic receptivity. You might imagine that a bunch of brightly colored helium balloons—red ones, blue ones, green ones, any of your favorite colors—are all tied by a string to their wrist. Truly seeing and feeling them lifting your arm with self-talk and images you create, soon you may feel a seemingly automatic rising of your arm. You might imagine them becoming bigger with each breath you take, causing your hand and arm to lift ever higher. The more colorful the description, the more vivid the image. When the arm seems to rise of its own accord, you have moved into hypnotic receptivity, likely the lighter alpha frequency of brain waves, and are ready then insert the predetermined image of the goal you have. If the arm drops, this means you are not in a hypnotic state and the image of the goal will not likely take hold. You can invent any image to create an arm levitation. Sometimes I imagine a strap around my wrist going up to a block and tackle on a tree and down to a wooden handle for my left hand to pull. When my left hand pulls, my right arm automatically goes up and I know I am ready for my directive. Another favorite version of this is to imagine I am lying in a shallow river I know and I allow my outstretched arm to move slightly up and down in the current.

Another way to use the ideomotor neuron activation is with a string and paper clip. Hold it dangling down between your finger and thumb and imagine the clip going in a circle without actually using any muscles. When you are able with practice to get it moving, you know you are in a light trance state. If you can keep it moving while you then imagine deeply your preconceived goal, you saved yourself a hypnotherapist fee. With daily practice you can give yourself suggestions like being comfortable in a cold shower and then prove that it worked to help create more confidence in the process.

Utilize All Five Senses when Developing Imagery

When we think of imagery, we often think only of visual imagery. However, imagery can also involve the senses of touch, taste, hearing, and smell. In fact, when several senses are combined, images tend to be more vivid. For example, you might be more apt to respond to an image of being relaxed by the ocean if you can feel the warm sand, hear the ocean waves crashing into the shore, smell the seaweed and kelp, taste the salty mist, and see the blue skies, and green frothy ocean. Imagery works best when you use positive images from your own experiences. Relying on scripts from the Internet may or may not serve you. A place that is relaxing to one person is not necessarily going to be relaxing to someone else.

Use Positive and Emotional Words

Besides being descriptive, your words should have an emotional, exciting intonation and emphasis. It is not known exactly why this increases the imagery potential, but it is thought that it relates to early childhood imagination experiences. Thus, instead of saying to yourself, "Your heart is beginning to beat more regularly now," say "*All* the fibers of your heart muscle are beginning to work *together* now as a *team, pumping fresh, oxygenated blood* to *all* of the cells in your body." The tone of excitement and emotion in your voice will intensify appropriate images and will also seem to validate them.

Keep words positive. Words like *not* or *won't* do not form images in the mind; therefore, images are produced by the object of the sentence that uses them. Directives that contain negations should therefore always be re-phrased.

Wrong way: You're not afraid any more.
Right way: You're feeling confident.
Wrong way: In a few moments you won't feel like crying.
Right way: In a few moments you will feel more relieved.

Wrong way: Don't breathe so fast.
Right way: Breathe slower.
Wrong way: You are not going to die.
Right way: You are going to live.

The following example demonstrates this point: A golfer wants to hit the ball down the fairway in between two ponds. If she says to herself, "Don't hit the ball in the pond," or "I will not hit the ball in the pond," what happens? The image-producing quality of the words *pond, hit,* and *ball* overshadows the (non-image-producing) word *not.* This is simply because the word "pond" is easier to visualize than the word "not." As a result, subtle body messages will tend to hit the ball into the pond as imagined. If, however, the golfer says to herself, I will hit the ball onto *the fairway,* she is more likely to do so.

Words with negative connotation should also be avoided. The most common such word used in communication with emergency patients is *pain.* Since any phrase that uses the word *pain* is still going to nurture the image, it is better to choose a word like *discomfort.* By using the word *discomfort* instead of *pain,* it is usually easier to be effective in not feeling "pain" but rather more comfortable. The directive or suggestion might "Notice how much *more comfortable* you are becoming."

Make Directives Relatively Believable

"Relatively believable" means being as honest and accurate as possible with the words you use to help create the images that can change your brain. Otherwise, you can use metaphors like little people on white horses for white blood cells. If you want to enhance your immune system, there is no need to talk about T cells and theta brain states. It would be sufficient to speak of immune cells banding together to rid the body of infection, while other cells relax.

Use the Progressive Form of the Present Tense
When Phrasing Directives

An example of languaging effectively might be if you are trying to stop your bleeding. Although a direct imperative like "Stop your bleeding *now*" can be effective, directives are more likely to be effective if they are phrased to give the patient more leeway to accept the appropriate images; for example, "Your arm is already beginning to feel numb," or "Notice that your arm is beginning to feel numb." This type of phrasing suggests that the patient should become aware of something that is already happening but she may not have noticed it yet. With this approach, there is less chance that the victim will resist a directive. There is also less chance that rapport will be lost because something you said did not happen right away. Instead, the patient has time to work up to the image. Forming directives in the present progressive also helps prevent the patient from trying too hard to comply. Another basic tenet of psychology is the law of reversed effect. This says that the harder you try to do something, the more likely it is you will fail. A directive like "Lower your body temperature, now," may increase activity in the left brain where willful determination is initiated. However, in the absence of strong, positive success images, willful determination somehow reinforces images that relate to the difficulty or inability to be successful. For instance, the harder you try not to blush, the more likely it is you will blush. Present progressive directives *assume* success, rather than demand it.

Make Directives Relative to You, Not the Environment

Of course your hypnosis can only apply to your thinking and behaviors in the world. Eventually you may be able to offer your help to others by teaching them what you have learned, but your directives can only relate to what you want to change or do in your life. Although in the Indigenous worldview there is ultimately no separation between you and your environment, hypnotic directives work when they are specific to your own ability to control something.

Wrong way: Notice how much cooler it is outside.
Right way: Notice how much cooler you feel.

On the other hand, there is evidence that when one becomes masterful with trance work, some people are able to use it to transfer healing energy to others. The Institute of Noetic Sciences has done a number of research studies on distant healing and subtle energy transfer.[19] Although this is worth mentioning as relates to our goals for healing the world, this book focuses only on what you can do to use trance and Indigenous worldview to change yourself so you can help the world. Sending deeply held prayers into the world and engaging the spirit world in dialogue while in trance can make a difference but we must start with ourselves.

Remember Words Are Understood More Literally

Notice in Step #2 of the Menninger protocol, there is mention of how words are taken literally. For directives to achieve the desired results, remember that one's words will be interpreted quite literally by trance logic. Images are stimulated by the perception of their initial meanings. Analytical brain functions that might otherwise be able to put the word or words into context are not operating during stress. This also means you want to make sure directives describe *activity,* not *ability.* For example, telling yourself, "Notice that you have the ability to stop your bleeding," is not as effective as saying, "Notice that your bleeding is beginning to stop." If you accept the image of the first directive you will indeed believe you have the ability to stop bleeding, but the mind will not direct the body to do it. Similarly, the use of the word *try* should be avoided because of the literal translation. Only when your directive says, "You are breathing more regularly," (direct) or "You are beginning to breathe more regularly" (present-progressive), will the desired objective occur.

Give Yourself a Post-Hypnotic Trigger

A *trigger* is a symbolic action that reintroduces a helpful image automatically. For example, you say, "Whenever I touch my finger and thumb together, the feeling of comfort will quickly and automatically return." Shrugging the shoulders, smiling, taking a deep breath, blinking the eyes, and so on can serve as triggers. Triggers are useful when there is a lack of confidence with the process or old mind programs are especially strong and the reminder can help trigger the original imagery without having to go into trance again when you are in the throes of a situation.

Hypnosis Work and the Ecological Crises

As stated in the Introduction, I wrote this book for two essential reasons: (1) to remind people that we have access to a proven and significantly different way of understanding our place in the world that can better lead to personal, social, and environmental well-being; and (2) to counter the belief that the worldview under which most of us operate evolved with the intention to make us forget the worldview that proved humans can live in relative harmony amongst ourselves and all other life forms. Under the Indigenous worldview, use of trance is a natural, continual part of living, communicating, and healing and it can help with both of these goals.

The human animal is a microcosm of the Planet Earth. We are made of the same mixtures of water and minerals. We both have great adaptability, yet our health depends upon a harmonious balance of many natural systems. The images we believe in are in many ways what manifest in the world. Because trance states are spontaneous and we are often unaware of how we and others are literally hypnotizing ourselves, we may be creating much of the destruction around us. We create a world that gives us evidence to support the imaginings by which we live.

It has been said that we are not suffering an energy crisis, but an intelligence crisis. Perhaps it would be more accurate to call it an imagery crisis. Just as negative images can negate survival mechanisms in the emergency patient, negative images can also create a self-fulfilling prophecy for the planet. Similarly, as positive images can create optimal survival and healing conditions for the mind-body complex, such images may be able to influence the health of the planet. If the analogy about humans and the earth is not sufficiently convincing—or if you have difficulty comparing between the influence of communication on the autonomic nervous system and the influence of communication on pollution, the depletion of natural resources, or war—consider the logic of physics.

The new physics reveals that energy is not constant, but rather manifests in lumps and bumps called *quanta*. These *quantum* gaps and jumps in the energy continuum defy our ordinary perception of space and time. They connect actions, places, ideas, and moments in ways that no one has been able to explain adequately. In fact, these quantum are so intimately interrelated that the eminent physicist Sir Arthur Eddington stated, "When the electron vibrates, the universe shakes." But how does quantum mechanics support the hypothesis that image-producing communication can affect the health of the planet? First of all, we must also note that the new physics views consciousness as a form of energy. Consciousness too, then, is interrelated with all actions, places, ideas, and moments. Since by consciousness we are linked to everything, we also influence everything. Just as the atoms that comprise our cells are interrelated with the atoms that comprise all other structures, our thoughts are thus interactive with all other structures. The British physicist, Sir James Jeans, described it well as far back as in the 1930s:

> Today there is a wide measurement of agreement...that the stream of knowledge is heading toward a nonmechanical reality; the universe begins to look more like a great thought than like a great machine. Mind no longer appears as an accidental intruder into the realm of matter; we are beginning to suspect that we ought rather to hail it as the creator and governor of the realm of matter. (137)

Another way to understand the effect of your thoughts and images on the universe around us is to recall how our own negative mood can affect people with whom you come in contact. Similarly, remember how your good mood can have a positive effect. Note that words and body language as well as your mood and thoughts triggered the reactions. All of this is to say that, through our thoughts, images, and daily communication, each of us has a way to alter the course of events that shapes the world picture. Unfortunately, most of us express our communication in a negative way. How easy this is to do when so many horrible things are being communicated to us through the media. Reports of ozone layer disruption; the greenhouse effect; food, water, and air pollution; traffic problems and crime; energy crisis; and war are heard or read almost daily. I started this book with reference to our being amidst a probable sixth extinction. When we respond to these reports, however, we do not have to join in the negativity. We can reframe the problem and change the images that are being projected.

For example, imagine you have just returned from a hectic commute in traffic. When you arrive home you read in the newspaper that the number of automobiles in your area will double in two years. Then you hear on the radio that pollution from auto exhausts is most responsible for the depletion of the ozone layer. At this point you could easily say to yourself something negative about the future of the planet, like, "Man, in five years we're not going to be able to breathe the air outside our door!" Yet with this statement you contribute to the self-fulfilling prophesy that many others are probably duplicating at the same moment. If, however, you prefer to reframe the problem as a challenge or an opportunity with a hopeful conclusion, you might say,

> You know, the pollution from automobiles has been getting worse each year. I'm going to do something to make the situation better. I read about an inventor who is trying to develop the capability to economically use helium as a fuel for cars so that the exhaust would be pure oxygen. Wouldn't it be amazing if the air got better because of automobile exhaust instead of worse? We will find an alternative when we're able to move beyond our mechanistic perspectives and recognize our interconnectedness and the power we can access.

If trance-based learning has any merit at all, then this simple reframing if done by enough people can create an environment in which discovering new solutions to the pollution problem will be significantly more likely; at some point the reframing process will engage hypnotic effects and penetrate our collective psyche. In addition to rephrasing the bad news into an opportunity for positive change, there is more you can do to optimize your images for the health of the planet. Moreover, when joined with those of others, the positive images you hold are transformational when reflected on with all modes of consciousness and put into action.

A recent experiment mentioned briefly in a previous note was conducted by one of my doctoral students at Fielding Graduate University for her doctoral dissertation on the use of nature films. Joo-Yeon (Christina) Ri supports the idea that too much concern with the catastrophes that may lie ahead, combined with not enough imagining the beauty of nature and positive possibilities, may actually move us away from our goal. Using the largest and most state-of-the-art MRI machine in the world, located at a medical university in South Korea, Joo-Yeon had subjects watch portions of Al Gore's alarming (but nonetheless important) documentary on global warming while in an MRI machine recording their brain activity. Then the subjects watched a simple "sights and sounds" of nature film Joo-Yeon had produced, depicting natural, pleasant, everyday images of healthy natural environments and creatures. During the watching of Gore's documentary, high levels of brain activity revealed deep cognitive thinking. The hypothalamus and pituitary centers stimulated the release of stress hormones while watching and listening to the dire predictions of what might happen if we do not take effective action soon. However, when the simple nature film was watched, cognitive functions were largely absent. Visual and auditory functions were minimal. This calming was accompanied by activity in the fibers communicating between the right and left hemispheres via the corpus callosum, indicating not only a relative lack of stress but also a healthy balance between left and right brain.

This is only very preliminary information and in itself may not offer much in terms of concrete conclusions. However, if watching the second film also tends to motivate people to be in and enjoy the natural world as Joo-Yeon theorizes, then her additional research—pointing to the idea that we are more likely to take care of nature if we spend more time appreciating it—may indicate that a focus on the positive is more motivational than the focus on the negative. This does not mean we shouldn't pay attention to the negative consequences; but only once we're aware, our psychological focus might better target the benefits of a healthy planet. Remember, in both spontaneous and intended trance, words are literally understood and programmed.

All of this does not point toward "positive thinking" nor hiding our heads in the sand. It is about accepting responsibility for reciprocity while at the same time seeing the beauty all around. Do not avoid bad news by trying to evade it. Become educated in alternatives for positive change so you can focus your internal images and communication. Remain open-minded. Trust your intuition as much as your logic. Here are some suggestions that can help in achieving this balance, that will work especially as part of a continual flow between waking reality and the spirit world, such as in between cognitive thinking and trance-oriented awareness:

1. *Tune in.* Literally stop to smell the flowers. Find a place that seems to have good energy and go there to watch the sunset. Tune into what is happening with all your senses. Allow boredom or anxiety to come and go. Notice your connection to sounds and sights of every dimension. If you see a creature, see it as a relation.

2. *Search for the hopeful viewpoint when you read or listen to radio or TV, while at the same time recognizing the likely hegemony intended to serve only a few at the expense of many.* The positive perspective may not be easy to find, but you will be surprised at how often you might have missed it in the past. More importantly, investigate the origins of your negative beliefs. Remember that beliefs are the foundation of images. If your beliefs are based on old bias or propaganda, your images will tend to perpetuate the negative effect of these ideas.

3. *Pay attention to your self-talk.* You communicate hundreds of words to yourself, without selectivity, every few minutes. Some of these words reinforce negative emotions and beliefs about yourself and the world. Listen to yourself and change the negative self-statements to positive ones.

4. *Utilize the power of repetition.* It is no secret why most of us use the same words to complete the sentence, "Things go better with _____." You do not need a multimillion dollar budget, however, to repeat optimistic statements to yourself or others often enough for them to take hold of your imagination.

5. *Take time when you do your personal consciousness work to focus specifically on something for the planet and other-than-human life.* Most of us use such opportunities to manage our stress, enhance our performance, or prepare for a crisis. We tend to leave the fate of the planet out of our positive images. Once in a while, take a few minutes and use self-hypnosis-type mental processes to create a positive image for the world. Be general, or use your knowledge to focus on specific solutions.

6. *Practice self control by using concentrative states as often as possible.* For example, see how long you can stand under an ice-cold shower without being bothered. Or, if you are ticklish, see if you can allow yourself to be tickled without tightening your muscles or laughing.

7. *Find a way to meditate that suits you.* There are many traditions available today that stem from shamanistic roots, and anything, from om chanting to yoga to simply watching and listening to Nature, can serve to enhance you and your community in magical ways.

8. *Interact with Nature.* We live on Earth. Trees, oceans, "wildlife," and exposure to storms and sunsets are vital to our energy expression. All the meditation or yoga or hypnosis or martial arts we can do cannot replace a walk in the woods, an adventure in a wilderness

environment, or a communion with the clouds or local birds. Experience nature and risk adventure in order to truly feel you are part of the universe.

9. *Emphasize love with self-hypnotic work.* Incorporate love into all of your personal trance-based learning, remembering the importance of treating all life with compassion and caring, including plants and rivers. Do not accept the premise that only humans have intrinsic value or that we are superior to all other creatures. Give your time and your energy to others, and remember to start with your inner circle of family and friends. Love yourself also, and love every moment as though it were your last, while maintaining a humility that never makes you feel superior to anyone.

10. *Remember to think in the present progressive tense.* By "becoming" in the now you remain in control. We have no control over the past or the future, only in some degree over the present. Although you can have images of a positive future, and you can review pleasant memories of the past, your mental concentration is the most effective when images are "becoming alive now."

11. *Constantly practice developing your intuition.* For example, if the phone rings, hesitate before answering and sense who it might be or what it might be about.

12. *Be positively motivated.* Visualize positive outcomes rather than avoiding negative ones.

13. *Do not give up.* Be persistent. Do not be disappointed if your positive attitude does not seem to change the world. All worthwhile efforts take time (perhaps a lifetime) and persistence.

14. *Be responsible.* We are individually responsible for how we respond to events and information. There is no benefit in just blaming others. If you think a corporation is doing something damaging to the environment, take some positive action. Each of us is accountable to life. We must decide on what values we attach to it, plan on ways to uphold those values, and set goals that actualize those values. Even if your goals are never fully realized, your continual pursuit of them makes you a role model for others to follow until their goal is ultimately accomplished. Taking responsibility also means doing what you can to optimize your own physical health. Proper exercise and nutrition habits combined with avoiding harmful substances and practices show that you are a responsible person. How can you effectively complain about industrial pollution if you continue to pollute your own body?

15. *Finally, carefully consider how the subjects of the next chapter (listed below) relate to the worldview precepts you currently hold in contrast with Indigenous ones, and how they in turn can positively affect trance-based learning.*

If you do not truly understand fear as an opportunity to practice a virtue, authority as only coming from honest reflection on lived experience, words as sacred vibrations that demand authenticity and care, art and music as essential processes of life like breathing, complementarity as a natural imperative, and nature as the ultimate teacher, then any use of trance-based learning will fall short of our ultimate goals.

Notes

1. Interestingly, I wrote a book published in 1998, the year after Ruiz published his, that was also based on a near-death experience. (For me it was being sucked into an underground hole on the Rio Urique during a kayaking expedition.) It also caused me to eventually learn from the Raramuri shamans of Mexico. Based on my doctoral dissertation, I introduce the four worldview precepts described in this book in much greater detail. See *Primal Awareness: A True Story of Survival, Awakening, and Transformation with the Raramuri Shamans of Mexico*. Mine did not sell five million copies. However, what I share in this book may be necessary for Ruiz's four agreements to truly take hold for personal and global transformation.
2. They include being impeccable with your word; not making assumptions; not taking things personally and always doing your best.
3. I also refer to this as "Concentration-Activated Transformation" or "CAT."
4. Although there is much controversy about what is or is not Toltec, the source Ruiz gives for his work, it is certainly possible that the wisdom of pre-contact people referred to by Maya and Aztec People could have been handed down orally to his grandfather. Scholars such as Susan D. Gillespie maintained that the difficulties in salvaging historic data from the Aztec accounts of Toltec history are too great to overcome. For more information see Gillespie, Susan. The Aztec Kings. University of Arizona Press and Davies, Nigel. The Toltecs. University of Oklahoma Press
5. Hypnosis when described as a state of consciousness is akin to trance, but is generally induced via passive relaxation and concentrations in this state that alter normal brain patterns. Usually it implies another person has been responsible for bringing you into this state and then offering appropriate directives to "reprogram" beliefs, abilities and behaviors. I prefer "trance-based learning" only because it is more amendable to self-hypnosis strategies of all sorts, including those that are anything but relaxing, as in vigorous dancing with purpose and vision.
6. Co-conscious means that other than and more than human entities not only have a consciousness of some design but that whatever it is can communicate with ours.
7. A number of studies show the life-enhancing hypnosis effect relates to changes in brainwave frequencies, with theta relaxation being most powerful. For example, Elmer and Alyce Green have for years in their laboratory at the Menninger Foundation studied the relationship between trance effects on brain-

wave activity and creativity. Their research shows that people can learn to slow their brainwave frequencies as they enter a trance and tap into high levels of creative thinking. However, further studies indicate additional factors and we remain far from fully understanding the nature and power of trance.

8. In her University of Texas dissertation, "Category Learning Systems," Dagmar Zeithamova concluded that at least four category learning systems exist, based on four memory systems of the brain: working memory, procedural memory, declarative memory and perceptual memory. The four categories of learning systems may compete or cooperate, each dominating within a different category of learning task.

9. Dr. Steven Gilligan, a Stanford-trained psychologist and specialist in hypnosis who worked closely with Milton Erickson, offers a definition for what he calls "generative trance" that comes close to Indigenous trance-based learning. He writes, "Generative trance is a higher state of consciousness wherein new identities and realities may be created. This state allows consciousness to unbind itself from the fixed settings of the conscious mind and re-attune to the infinite possibilities of the creative unconscious, thereby making possible the reorganization of the mental filters underlying reality construction." He also understands co-conscious dimensions, which I address shortly.

10. It is likely that Indigenous knowledge of plants is a co-conscious phenomenon. Knowing which combinations of plants affect specific organs result from direct communication with plants. Similarly, traditional hunter-gatherers used trance to communicate with animals they would hunt in ways that helped assure both success and a willingness of sorts for the animal to offer his body during the hunt.

11. In *Primal Awareness*, I describe how I came about this new approach. It was after a near-death experience I had in a kayaking adventure in Mexico and a vision that came to me while in a trance state.

12. Caught on film, it looked even more lethal when I watched it on television the following week because of the dramatic music that they used when he was rearing. Interestingly, another time when I was doing a fire walk in my professional fireman's uniform, CBS news filmed it. For me it was another opportunity to demonstrate trance phenomenon. For CBS it was the image of a local firefighter walking on fire. When it was aired on the 11 PM news, a good four hours after the event, CBS had also added dramatic music while the camera was focused on my bare feet walking across the smoldering 1500 degree centigrade embers. While my comrades and I watched the clip, I felt a hot pain on the bottom of my foot and quickly undid my laces and pulled off my boot. Caught up in the dramatic imagery and music while watching myself step on the coals, a blister suddenly emerged!

13. The martial artists of China and elsewhere train to master the power of *qi*, in essence an energy source that stems from the power of trance. They are able to tap into this automatically and quickly when needed (Yuasa et al).

14. See for example, *Biology of Belief* by Bruce Lipton. His work has become very popular, but few know of his deep interest in Indigenous worldview. We met this year at a Cree Sun Dance where he was a helper in preparation and ceremony for those of us who danced.

15. There are religious sects that use trance in different ways and people are often entranced by religions by external authorities. Polarities between "god" and "devil" bring fear into the equation. The Raramuri Simerones of Mexico have shamans called *Sukuruames* who because of their knowledge of trance work have great powers. If one becomes greedy or otherwise misuses his or her powers they just ban or boycott the person and disregard him. However, the same Indians who live higher up in the canyon and have adopted Christian beliefs such as relating to good and evil, God and Devil, have a different reaction to the power-hungry shaman. They begin to fear him and see him as a sorcerer.

16. For a thorough and up-to-date study and evidence of the placebo phenomenon, visit Harvard Medical School's website to access 85 peer-reviewed publications from between 1998 to 2014: http://programinplacebostudies.org/publications/

17. One of my former students did a dissertation showing that in the absence of stress, a focus on natural sights and sounds of nature while in an MRI machine creates activity in the corpus callosum to implement complementarity. I was a participant and when I stepped out of the MRI, the neuroscientists who were monitoring things acted shocked when they looked at my brain scan. Thinking I had a brain tumor or something terrible, I asked what was their concern. They asked me how old I was and at the time I was 62 or 63. Apparently my own grey matter was tightly bound and thick as a much younger person's would be. Apparently my own hypnotic and meditative work coupled with my creative engagement with the natural world likely culminated in preventing the loss of grey matter with age that normally happens in the dominant cultures.

18. This induction approach has potential to bring you into the deeper theta state which arguably can be more powerful for personal transformation. However, a lighter state of alpha brain wave frequencies can accomplish much. I had abdominal surgery with a lighter state of trance. Next I'll describe a pendulum technique for lighter trance that also let's you know you are actually in the hypnotic receptivity needed for suggestions or directives to take hold.

19. Just Google "Distant Healing" and Subtle Energy Healing" along with "Institute of Noetic Sciences" to see their research.

2

Courage and Fearlessness

If you talk to the animals they will talk with you and you will know each other.
If you do not talk to them you will not know them and what you do not know
you will fear. What one fears, one destroys.

—Chief Dan George, Tsleil-Waututh Nation

Let me not pray to be sheltered from dangers, but to be fearless in facing them.

—Rabindranath Tagore

Fear and Trance

The relationship between trance-based learning and fear is an important one for us to understand because fear can make us receptive to hypnotic suggestions in ways that can be positive or negative. Like the wild mustang mentioned in the previous chapter, all creatures during times of significant stress become hyper-suggestible to the communication signals of a perceived trusted authority figure. I did not have the same success when I tried to use the same telepathic "horse whispering" approach on domesticated horses presumably because they were not so fearful of humans.

Point of Departure, pages 53–71

In animals and people, this automatic receptivity to external assistance when in the throes of fear lasts for less than an hour before previously learned beliefs create positive or negative responses (Jacobs). Any confident person who is first on the scene of a medical emergency can offer verbal instructions to a victim in spontaneous trance to control involuntary nervous system functions, like bleeding and blood pressure. If a rescuer is unaware of this receptivity and is perceived by the victim to be an authority figure, words can cause untold harm (American Academy of Orthopedic Surgeons 61).[1]

This potential problem has an analogy in the larger world. When we are afraid, we are susceptible to the repetitive or hypnotic mandates of the hegemons and their media or political functionaries. Over time, this has contributed to the success of educational hegemony as well. Such cultural and educational influence in behalf of corporate interest may be one of the best ways to explain the irrationality behind our destruction of vital life systems. Forgetting about or letting go of our trust and skill in using trance-based co-conscious learning allows others to manipulate our beliefs. Perhaps this is what happened to allow for our point of departure so long ago. Some charismatic leaders led us away from our trance-based lives. This is a theory that Julian Jaynes put forth in his classic text, *The Origin of Consciousness in the Breakdown of the Bicameral Mind*. Instead of listening to co-conscious entities via trance awareness during times of stress or confusion, we developed a consciousness that replaced our listening to the "voice of God" (or Nature) with listening to that of human kings.[2]

In any case, whether under Indigenous or dominant worldview, most cultures applaud the concept of courage. In the dominant cultures, we tend to make a big deal out of acts of courage when they make the news. Perhaps this reminds us that courage is still a main feature of human behavioral ideals. However, if we consider the daily practices of most people, it appears that courage has become a "weak sister."[3] When guided by uninvestigated authority amidst technological comfort and separation from nature, courage takes a back seat. In cultures of fear, whether under fascist rule or democracies supposedly threatened by outside forces, manifesting courage seems to have become either too dangerous or too inconvenient.

Courage and Western Philosophy

Such de-evolution should not surprise us. Most of our foundational Western philosophers have supported it. Aristotle for example spoke of courage in terms of moderation. He saw cowardice and recklessness as two ends of the courage spectrum. Reasoning was therefore the most important determinant of courage. According to this thinking, women could not be courageous because at the time he and most Greeks felt women were not good at reasoning. They were thus not candidates for being virtuous and could not be leaders or philosophers.

This contrasts with Indigenous understandings. In them, reasoning plays a role but there is much more to it. First, it is a creative power necessary for helping one's community and living in harmony with the environment. It is a mental/spiritual strength that allows people to venture forth in the face of great challenges even when the outcome is uncertain, sometimes in spite of reason. It incorporates passion, a deep concern for the greater good, and a profound sense of integrity, and it expresses trust in the universe. It could never be reckless or moderated toward cowardice. Instead of reason as a primary force, trance-based learning and interconnectedness with co-conscious learning was the key to this virtue. A sense of separateness rather than lack of reasoning is perceived as the ultimate cause of fear and realization of interconnectedness the strongest source of courage.

As for perspectives on women, they are generally considered to be the most courageous gender under Indigenous worldview. This is why when Lakota women Sundance they do not pierce as do the men. They already have the courage to face pain and death; natural possibilities relating to childbirth. Men have to continually relearn courage. Women have also always been regarded as important leaders in Indigenous communities. Oral traditions and primary sources document the centrality of women leadership. In addition to responsibilities relating to decisions about whether or not to go to war, they were always "planting chiefs, sensitive funeral directors, vision quest mentors, inventive chefs, elaborate quill and bead workers, nurturing parents, articulate judges, knowledgeable herbalists, and brilliant counselors" (Mann 129).

The famous father of Western philosophy, Socrates, restricted ideas about courage even more than Aristotle. For example, he did not think that the ability to face death in battle should be described by this virtue. After all, he reasoned, if you are in battle you expect to be killed and therefore do not fear it. If you do not fear it, according to his logic, you cannot have courage. Instead, Socrates believed that courage occurred primarily when it stood strong behalf of knowledge. This would make it a true virtue. Human knowledge, learned from dialogue amidst his fellow man, was the only thing worthy of bringing courage to this level.

The half-truths about courage put forward by Aristotle and Socrates continued with most of the early Western philosophers who followed until such pantheists as Spinoza and eventually Emerson and D. H. Lawrence came along as outliers.[4] They sustained the new worldview that replaced authentic courage with the pursuit of knowledge and subservience to authorities (the state). Life, relationships, and sustainability were sacrificed as a result. Today most of our fears relate to ego, social or economic injuries and instead of courageous resolution, modern humans explode with anger, put on blinders, escape through drugs or hope that soon enough "knowledge" will make things right. Historian Paul Woodruff puts this back on Socrates:

> Socrates spent too much time looking for the kind of knowledge[5] he would never achieve, and not enough looking for ways to live well without this knowledge." Socrates' failure of political courage was not a failure of character; he was not weak or wrongheaded. It was a failure endemic to philosophy itself, and this is its lesson for us. Positive courage in politics calls for us to take action even at times when we cannot be sure we are right—and those are exactly the times when Socrates would hold up his hand and cry for a pause, while elenchus (*an argument*) determined that we did not know enough to go forward. But events do not pause for philosophy.

Socrates, like most philosophers who have shaped, rationalized, or been influenced themselves by the dominant worldview did not rely upon other-than-human wisdom. Indigenous worldview sees courage as inseparable from a deep sense of relationship and reciprocity to all of life. "Other-than-humans" represent the ultimate teachers of courage and phenomenon that contributes to life's inherent beauty. Every life form from trees and rivers to insects and fish model varying degrees of courage or fearlessness. Lessons can be learned from the lone tree growing out of a boulder, separated from its brothers and sisters in the fertile woods below but still strong and vibrant. Not all trees can survive such an environment; only those with courage. A golden eagle refusing to let go of its mountain goat prey as they tumble dangerously down the cliffs together does so not because of desperate starvation or genetic imperative but as an act of courage. It does not take many observations of salmon making their way straight up a waterfall in spite of looming black bears reaching out to grab them to feel their great courage and determination. And what of the bears themselves, balancing 30 feet in the air alongside rushing water?

We may think that such examples are not really courage because we assume reasoning and choice are not involved and believe that these are necessary for such acts to be called courageous. Yet I have seen young bears afraid to go to the edge of the waterfall to catch salmon. They must be taught the courage. If they learn it and go to the ledge as adults then it seems that some form of "choice" is a part of the process. I have seen a baby bald eagle "afraid" to jump out of its nest high in a cedar tree until the mother pushed it out. Do they learn courage also? I do not know if salmon are taught courage in preparation for their return to give birth, but some seem more determined and persistent than others. There is an African proverb, "The little ant at his hold is full of courage" and another that says, "The tiny ant dares to enter the lion's ear." I doubt that such Indigenous observations merely anthropomorphize animals in light of most Native beliefs that would tend to discourage this practice. Anyone who has owned a pet dog, cat, or parrot knows they can feel fear and yet, with encouragement, they overcome it. Is this only because of some imperative of instinct? Or might we give more credit to other-than-humans for their displays of courage and fearlessness as a learned phenomenon also? (We answer this in the final chapter on Nature.)

Indigenous Courage Today

My references to Indigenous courage are not relegated to the past or to their famous courage in battle. Indigenous People, like the early Greeks before Socrates, saw a willingness to face death in battle as one manifestation of courage. Courage was not so much aligned with killing as it was with risking death for the greater good. The practice of "counting coup" done by some American Indian tribes demonstrated a way to display personal courage by risking a charge against an enemy to merely touch him and not try to kill him. In spite of their courage in battle being significant, I wish to minimize the commonly acknowledged courage of Indigenous warriors in battle for three reasons.

First, the highest expression of courage under Indigenous worldview is generosity. Imagine a child giving her prize puppy to another more needy child and you get the idea of the potential relationship between courage and generosity. Many philosophers have said that love is the opposite of fear, at least once fear has served its immediate survival function of fight or flight. Generosity is the manifestation of love. As cowardice, panic, withdrawal, and other behaviors react to fear, generosity is the physical reaction to love. This morning I was listening to Amy Goodman's interview with Albert Woodfox on DemocracyNow.org. Woodfox was released from prison on February 19, 2016 after 43 years in solitary confinement, more than anyone else in U.S. history. Likely the result of his organizing a chapter of the Black Panther Party to address horrific conditions in Louisiana's Angola prison and helping to stop the sexual slave trade going on there. When Goodman asked him how he survived, he said

> One of my inspirations was Mr. Nelson Mandela. You know, I learned from him that if a cause was noble, you could carry the weight of the world on your shoulder. I thought that standing up for the weak, protecting people who couldn't protect themselves, was a noble cause. . . . You know, we were not fighting for the prison, be were fighting for society, we were fighting for all the injustices that happened in America and around the world. (transcript of 2/22/16)

The second reason Indigenous courage was not just about behaviors in warfare is because warfare in pre-contact times was minimal or absent in most Indigenous cultures (Leavitt, Van der Dennen, Bower) as it is in most surviving ones (Peacfulsocieties.org). Third, Indigenous courage is not an artifact of the past. It is represented today perhaps more than ever as Indigenous Peoples struggle to save the last pristine places on the planet, places inhabited by Indigenous Peoples and threatened by neoliberal forces.

In spite of the numbers of Indigenous individuals who have finally succumbed to the constant assault on their language, values, homeland, livelihood and identity, many communities have managed to hold on to their worldview. They continue to be the most vibrant models for authentic courage today. They remain on the frontline battles against oil companies and other assaults on air, land, water, and fellow creatures, facing death by hired thugs (Global Witness). In *Indigenous Encounters with Neoliberalism, Place, Women and the Environment in Canada and Mexico,* Isabel Altamirano-Jimenez shows how Indigenous Peoples describe this courage and how women are often leading the way. Story after story can be told about the courageous efforts of such Indigenous activists. In the Amazon Rain Forest the Achuar and other tribes are risking their lives to protect their homes and traditional territories from oil extraction, mining, mega-dam construction, logging, and other threats. In Canada, Guatemala, Papua New Guinea, Botswana , the Philippines, Nova Scotia, South Dakota similar battles are occurring. Throughout Mexico many Indigenous communities are struggling for social and ecological justice.

One of the tribes of Mexico I have had the honor of spending time with is the Raramuri who are also called Tarahumara. As with most Indigenous perspectives they see courage as being a vital aspect of life's inherent beauty. In varying degrees, they believe every living thing from trees and rivers to insects and fish demonstrate courage. Courage is part of the soul of Grandmother Earth. In Raramuri language *iwi* is the root word for soul and means breathing and life. They believe their own souls determine their physical, mental, and emotional vitality. This vitality is revered and is often expressed with phrases like the imperative *iwe'rasa,* meaning "Be determined, don't back down or give up!" Another common phrase is *siwe'ma,* which means, "Don't be disheartened" or "Don't be afraid." The essence of life for the Raramuri, in spite of centuries of genocidal oppression that continues today is associated with going forward in the face of fear.

The Ojibwa come to mind as having similar ideas about soulful courage as the Raramuri. In the Anishinaabe language, *Aakode'ewin* literally means "state of having a fearless heart" and "to do what is right even when the consequences are unpleasant" (Benton-Banai 47). The anthropologist Michael Cepek, who studied the Cofán, wrote, "distinct conceptions of fearlessness structure the complex relationships" that have allowed them to take on the many challenges they face (Cepek 334).

The legacy of such courage is in all of our potentialities, but we have allowed our post-point of departure worldview to be overshadowed by science and religion. In *The Rainbow Tribe: Ordinary People Journeying on the Red Road*, Ed McGaa (Eagle Man) writes about how too many teachers, religious fundamentalists and scientists have "buried their heads in the sand." He continues, "Their lack of courage teaches me why the old-time Sioux declared this virtue (courage) on of the four cardinal virtues needed to be a truly beneficial two-legged on one's earth journey." I know Eagle Man and he does not just write about courage. As a Marine Corps pilot, he returned from 110 combat missions in Viet Nam to dance in six annual Sioux Sun Dances and, like many other Lakota, he has dedicated much of his life to helping the world regain its balance by understanding our original Indigenous knowledge.

A number of contemporary Western thinkers recognize the nature of Indigenous courage as something special. The Smithsonian Institute's critical review of Dee Brown's history of the American west, *Bury My Heart at Wounded Knee*, says that understanding the truth about Indigenous Peoples "counters the stereotype of 'ignorant' or 'savage' Indians, and the courageous spirit they reveal evokes admiration and respect" (Anthropology Outreach). Noam Chomsky said the same thing in his 1992 booklet, *What Uncle Sam Really Wants*: "The courage they show is quite amazing. It's a very moving and inspiring experience, and brings to mind some contemptuous remarks of Rousseau on Europeans who have abandoned freedom and justice for the peace and repose they enjoy in their chains" (100). More recently, he spoke before the Second National Mexican National Congress of Indigenous and Intercultural Education about "the courageous teachers in Oaxaca," whose struggle "of enormous significance " counters the stereotype of "ignorant" or "savage" Indians, and the courageous spirit they reveal evokes admiration and respect.

Such education about ways to understand fear and courage continues to be a sign of hope. The development of courage should be a primary goal for learning. A vital tool for building compassion and self-discipline, it is the foundational virtue for moral education and that it can be taught via Indigenous worldview is an important realization. Julie Davis reveals evidence for this in Survival Schools: The American Indian Movement and Community Education in the Twin Cities. It is about two actual schools created by AIM to rescue Indigenous worldview. I was struck by how many graduates of the schools the author named who became truly courageous adults, manifesting their courage (and likely their fearlessness) on many paths. Many if not most of the students who attended had not been raised according to Indigenous worldview, but this virtue was rekindled in their hearts nonetheless. This realization of such possibilities encouraged me to write this chapter.

Of course, the Survival Schools lasted only a short while. When the Reagan administration came to power the funding for the two schools evaporated. There are still schools around the world, however, teaching Indigenous courage. For example, consider the education in Africa of the Chagga People and how it relates to this chapter's topic.

> In Indigenous philosophy, courage means the strength of spirit that enables people to accept the unavoidable tragedies of life without being disintegrated. It implies the readiness and willingness to take certain reasonable risks for the good of family and community. One is not obliged to take unreasonable risk or be careless in the face of danger but *Ko moowu kokyefiiro pvo* (means) there is no wailing (a mournful cry announcing a death) in the home of one who runs away from danger. Equally unpopular is the person who will not dream dreams or dare to adventure into a new enterprise or course of action or the one who postpones decision making for too long. *Kwilike* is a name meaning one who courageously stands on one's own feet, the fearless one ... It was understood to reflect the moral strength and determination to keep on a chosen course of action to achieve one's ends; the ability to hold on to one's morale when opposed or threatened; patience and unwillingness to accept defeat prematurely; spiritual strength to positively go through hardships and tragedies; and the readiness to take reasonable risk for personal or common good. It is one of the fundamental virtues that helps Indigenous societies grow and thrive. (Mosha 128)

Fearlessness and "The Great Mysterious"

Most of the education about Indigenous worldview that incorporates the importance of courage does not say much about fearlessness. Nonetheless, Indigenous worldview holds that courage leads to fearlessness at a magical point when the commitment to act on the courage is irrevocable. It is about a kind of trust in the universe that is a legacy for all of us. We face a situation in the world that demands that we re-embrace this perspective as best we can. Fearlessness ultimately helps promote courageousness because it neutralizes the stress of practicing courage which ultimately diminishes our consistent employment of it. (Perhaps this is why so many courageous activists I know burn out.) If fearlessness does not follow courage while one is taking a virtuous action in the face of the feared consequences, sustaining courage implies a continuing focus on the fear as well. Over time, this can cause some degree of hesitation in going forward with courageous actions. It can set up a reluctance to suffer through it again and again that prevents it from becoming a way of life.

Such ideas stand in stark contrast to what psychologist, philosophers and website searches reveal about fearlessness. They either refer to it as merely a synonym for courage or they rebuke it as being a form of apathy, over-confidence, arrogance or ignorance. "Only fools are not afraid" is an oft seen quote, one I remember from my own military training in the Marines. Such perspectives are half-truths from the Indigenous perspective. Of course one must have an initial sense of danger or risk when faced with it. When we use courage, however, as an opportunity for practicing virtues in behalf of the greater good and with full acceptance of unknown outcomes, we can move into authentic fearlessness to achieve our greatest strength. Far from being unaware, we become more aware. We become fully alive in our realization of interconnectedness with all, including life and death, and content in our effort in behalf of the world.

Religious faith in a supreme God or "fear of God" has also evoked a form of fearlessness in people under the dominant worldview. Whether such fearlessness expresses holistic reasoning, a sense of interconnectedness, and a consistent effort in behalf of doing well in the world is fodder for another book. Still, if unquestioning orthodoxy and undoubting belief in one's salvation were the basis for such fearlessness, it would not serve virtue consistently. Fearlessness requires a deep trust in the universe when working in behalf of the greater good but it also requires a willingness to accept and embrace the unknown. Any fearlessness that is based on absolute human knowledge is going to be subject to some inner deception because none of us can know the full truth and deep down we know it.

This is why embracing of mystery and a willingness to admit to not knowing became part of the Indigenous worldview. Under it a commitment to humble unknowingness defines our relationship to everything. Instead of assuming we are at the mercy of a definable "Supreme Being" or "God," indigenous peoples rely on metaphorically defined energies to help direct healthful relationships in the world. It is likely that prehistoric indigenous language had no words at all for such a being (Cox). Rather a variety of verb-based words describing sacred energies expressed as an "oneness" of all things. We cannot know for sure if words used today handed down through oral tradition ever referred to a specific deity per se, but in any case the words used for what might be interpreted as some Supreme Creator still retain this sense of unknowing. For the Lakota, reference to the force of original creation uses the word *Wakan Tankan* that literally means "The Great Mysterious" and is conceived as an unexplainable power that manifests through countless beings, spirits, and matter. In *Ojibway* the word is *Kitchi Manitou* also translated as "Great Mystery." The Navajo have no specific words for what they conceive as an unnamable and unknown power whose spirit is in all creation. Similarly the Toltec concept for the energy behind creation translates to the concept of "oneness" Such agnosticism brought forth a more authentic ability to trust in the visible and invisible energies in the universe, not visa versa. And it takes a degree of fearlessness to embrace the unknown.

Gandhi seems to be an important exception to how the dominant religious beliefs use a supreme being (God) to support fearlessness. Perhaps this is partly because his religion, Hinduism, may have been most conducive to Indigenous worldview. It is the oldest of the historical written religions (Devadatta). Gandhi referred to his ideas about fearlessness as "the ancient path of truth and non-violence" (Gandhi). Hinduism allowed him to maintain his agnostic beliefs via the concept of *nirguna* that essentially referred to God as an indescribable force rather than as a being. It also was fully supportive of his sense about the importance of fearlessness since this idea heads the list of the Divine Attributes enumerated in its 16th Chapter of the Gita.

Whether Hinduism's close foundational ties or his independent intuitive and reasoned conclusion were responsible for his reclaiming Indigenous worldview, or some combination which is most likely, Gandhi's concept of fearlessness comes close to how it is perceived with Indigenous worldview. Both are about truth seeking and oneness as cooperative concepts. In his philosophy of nonviolent resistance he called *Satyagraha* there is no place for fraud or falsehood, or any kind of untruth, something rare in our post point of departure world but common in what Cooper refers to as "a time before deception" in his book about native worldviews. The connection between Gandhi's passion for truthfulness and fearlessness is an important link to Indigenous worldview especially because in he embraced *anekantavada*, a concept from Jainism, a religious tradition clearly based upon Indigenous spirituality. It described the contention that no person could ever know the whole truth but only partial truth.

In fact, a number of Indigenous worldview precepts weave through Gandhi's interpretation of and dedication to his religion that seem to support his passion for fearlessness (Veeravalli). He believed in the Vedas but did not see them as divine or absolute. He believed in the institution of the Guru in general, but did not think it vital to literally find and follow one. He believed that cow protection was symbolic of God's mandate to respect and protect all of life. He was skeptical of private ownership of land and fought for more commons for all to share without cost. He possessed no fear of death, placed priority on local issues, and emphasized peacefulness coupled with a fierce dedication to truthfulness. All of these ideas collectively reveal neither religious orthodoxy nor dominant worldview, but rather ways of seeing the world according to the Indigenous worldview.

Kujur's chapter in *The Meaning of Mahatma for the Millennium* fully supports this view, as does Devadattas. In Kujur's "Gandhian Thought Vis-à-vis Indigenous Ideology" he writes: "In spite of the fact that Gandhi was relatively passive towards the tribal causes, if one looks into the Gandhian philosophy and indigenous ideology, one cannot but be amazed by the extent to which they shared values, ethos and the spirit" (84). According to Kujur, Gandhi often spoke about *arvodaya* which meant "development of all," noting that Tribal society has evolved a sociocultural mechanism to take care of the entire tribe with "corresponding traditional tribal values of tolerance, harmony, equality, sharing, humility, honesty, simplicity and symbiosis with nature that are being looked upon as irrelevant today" (85).[6]

The role of our post-point of departure religions in creating a dependence on various forms of religious orthodoxy and fundamentalism in ways that may have reduced our ability to practice fearlessness deserves a little more space here. Dominant worldview and the world's historical religions are intricately connected and along with modern science have diminished our original priority on courage as well. To complete this argument, I refer the world's most notable professor of religious study, Huston Smith. The front matter of Smith's 2006 book *A Seat at the Table: In Conversation with Native Americans* reads "Not only is he one of the most widely respected scholars of religion in the world, he has also been a tireless advocate for Native Americans for the last twenty-five years" (Smith ix). I think Huston Smith's personal transformation from his devotion to the dominant worldview to being an advocate for the Indigenous one is significant.

For his entire career as a university professor of philosophy from 1944 until near his retirement in four decades later, Smith gave no noticeable attention to Indigenous spiritual traditions. His best selling book, *The Religions of Man*, published in 1958 and republished as *The World's Religions* in 1991 and again in 1998, sold more than two million copies. In the later edition he explains that he changed the name of the book because of the feminist movement. It is more likely a result of his awakening to the world-view of American Indians. After forty years of ignoring them, he added a chapter on "Primal Religions" in his new edition and writes in the foreword of the 50th Anniversary edition while at University of California Berkeley in 1998, "I am especially glad that I will not go to my grave having let stand a book on religions that omitted its primal, oral, tribal members" (xii). A little earlier, in the new preface for a second edition of his 1992 text, *Forgotten Truth: The Common Vision of the World's Religions,* he writes:

> The time is ripe for that correction and this is what prompts the new Preface to this book. Our mistake was expecting science to provide us with a worldview, when we now see that is shows us only half-the world-its physical, calculable, testable, significantly controllable, half. And even that half is now unpicturable. So science no longer presents us with a model for even half of the world....We have been in a tunnel so long one has forgotten that sun and stars and rain exist. The premodern realization that they do exist- that things more wonderful than the tunnel vision of modernity allowed are not only real but also more real than the ones that pushed them out of sight- is the thesis this essay explores with absolute seriousness. (vi)

Two events were likely catalysts for Smith. One related to his work with the Harvard Group and Timothy O'Leary with entheogenic plants, such as hallucinogenic plants used by Indigenous cultures for mystical purposes. Although he refers to this time as his "most spiritually meaningful days" in his book about his experiences, *Cleaning the Doors of Perception,* I can only suppose that the plant teachers more than his colleagues may have helped him realize the folly of his great disregard for Indigenous spirituality. A second event he tells in his latest edition of *The World's Religions* is about how after five decades of never having a single American Indian student in one of his classes, he had one in a lecture the day his brother died. He tells how the student came up to him after class and walked with him to his office, telling him that in his people's way, one sits with another who has lost a loved one. The young man sat in his office silently for 20 minutes then left.

> Then something happened. I started finding myself looking back toward to past. "It crept up on my quite surprisingly. It wasn't the new or the future. After 5 decades, I moved away from the west. All along I was looking for truth. Surprisingly, I came to understand there was more truth in the traditional than in the modern. There was more wisdom condensed in these enduring traditions than in the modern outlook. (xii)

In his book, *The Courage to Teach,* Park Palmer, a Quaker, defines truth-seeking as the ultimate goal of education. Like Gandhi and the Indigenous worldview, he also holds that truth is not relative but it is an eternal conversation. The story of Huston Smith's long history of missing what he now considers to be the most vital path to truth seeking owing to his ignoring of Indigenous worldview is a lesson for us all as is Palmer's idea that truth-seeking is all about courage, and ultimately, I contend, fearlessness.

Experiential Learning of Courage and Fearlessness

Both Gandhi and Smith used their genius for metacognition, their awareness of Indigenous worldview and practice in the real world as ingredients for their own transformative learning. We end this chapter by offering a teaching strategy for all three components. The approach I describe can be used not only with personal fears but for other life challenges as well. Note there are references to the topics covered in the next chapters, so you will be more proficient in doing this exercise after you read them. But consider them now in preparation for reading the rest and then return to the guidelines below again. Here are the first six metacognitive steps, one for each direction including the four cardinal ones, the sky, and the Earth.

Metacognition

1. Identify the fear or anxiety that if faced would make life better for all, and describe it. Have you used the usual post-point of departure approach to fear? Have you mostly ignored it or to avoided it? Do you prefer not to discuss it? Have you been unwilling to change it? Would it be better for you and the world if you could? Can you think of a time when you might have been in trance and the fear was planted somehow as a hypnotic suggestion? If so, can you describe what happened?

2. Whatever the fear is, what is the authority source that describes everything about it? What is the authorization for the fear, the rationale for it? How real, truthful, or accurate is it? If you were to honestly and courageously analyze it from only your life's experience, would the fear be worth keeping any longer? How has it stifled your positive potential in and for the world?

3. What words are associated with the fear? Are the words perfectly truthful and accurate? How can use describe it more accurately?

4. How has the fear represented itself as being or not being part of the Natural world? If it does not seem to relate to Nature, creatively search for a relationship or connection that is less obvious. Try to imagine a teaching from Nature that would teach you about the

fear and about how to overcome it. What is the teaching? If not, stay open to a forthcoming teaching from Nature within the next 48 hours. This could also relate to a real-life confrontation with the fear's trigger, known in psychology as an "in-vivo exposure."

5. Now enter into a light trance to imagine how you would rightfully respond to the fear's antecedents. Use self-hypnosis techniques you have learned or engage with intuitively selected music or other activities that will safely bring you to an alternative awareness. Have clear, positively phrased words memorized so you will not have to think about them when you are visualizing outcomes. Make sure the hypnotic image and verbal suggestion are sufficient to give you a relatively clear image and are relatively believable and possible. Remember that in trance your words become quite literal so phrase everyone with only positive words. Don't say " I will NOT be fearful," but rather, "I will be courageous" (or fearless depending on the circumstance). Deliver the message and engage the image with just the right amount of enthusiasm for its outcome. Not too much or too little.)

6. Within 24 hours, do something in the real world that can demonstrate your success in gaining either courage or fearlessness as relates to the original fear.

In-Vivo Exposure

"In Vivo Exposure" is a cognitive behavioral strategy that when used with imaginal therapy is a powerful intervention for overcoming fears from relatively minor anxieties to major phobias. It involves real-life confrontation with the source of the fear. It is too bad that "in vivo exposure" is thought of mainly as a psychological intervention. We learn from real-life experiences, yet civilization allows us to avoid those that make us uncomfortable. Anything we can do as a sort of praxis for learning can build character and make the six universal virtues of courage, honesty, fortitude, patience, humility, and generosity a part of our identity. Intention is key. Remember that once the immediate fight or flight response to fear is over, any continuing fear is to be seen as an opportunity for practicing one of these virtues. If you come upon a bear and it is not possible to run or fight, then practicing patience by seeing how long you can stand your ground with peaceful vibrations. Practice generosity by offering your berries or even yourself if the bear is hungry enough. Experience fearlessness and trust the universe and watch the bear walk away! Dominant culture too often uses fear as a controlling device instead of a character builder. This has made us afraid of Nature, seeking materialistic safety and convenience instead.

Indigenous stories about "monsters" that are really those potential barriers in ourselves to walking in balance to help teach youngsters about courage and fearlessness early on. (They were also used to warn about wrongdoing, but only as a very early strategy and one that would be revealed later.) Fears are still presented in stories, like fear of loss of identity, so that we may live our lives in ways that we can overcome them. It is natural to have some fear of death, of loss of family, of friends, of identity, and so on, and stories gave us hints as to how to be heroes of our own story. One way to accomplish this is through games. Through them we can confront a variety of ego-based fears by focusing on our positive physical, mental, social, creative and spiritual potentiality. In Indigenous communities, preparation via praying and singing and fasting and dancing so as to engage trance-based learning was common. According to Greg Cajete, in our chapter on "Fear and Courage" in *Critical Neurophilosophy and Indigenous Wisdom*:

> Native players strove to achieve the 'highest thought in their training and game playing. This ideal of the highest thought is a generic term for a commonly held set of values and belief for guiding the alignment of mind, body and spirit with high ethical and spiritual standards for training and participation. It was akin to the ideal of "sportsmanship" today but went much deeper in its personal and cultural implications. As an ideal it was something to be sought amidst the human challenges given the propensity of human beings to be also egotistical, vengeful, jealous and argumentative, as well as adaptive, persistent (games often lasted days), and in-balance. (56)

Just as I learned about going without water in the heat from a kangaroo rat, watching animals of all kinds was a primary way to learn the skills needed when playing. Indigenous players learned how to move physically and they learned how to cooperate as a team. They learned from animals how to flow with whatever circumstances appeared. Most important was finding and/or creating flowing balance. "Playing with all of one's heart usually requires some level of courage to face all sorts of fears. Ego attachment and the many fears relating to ego are overcome and achieved in such a way that during the players full involvement with the game, they 'forget themselves' and thereby become one with themselves" (Cajete 58).

The Xavante Indigenous People of Brazil play a game with similar purposes in mind. This one is a log race where runners take turns in relay fashion carrying a palm log on their shoulders. That one of the team's logs is much heavier would concern a typical sports fan, but not the Xavante. They would not understand such a concern. As the race goes on and the team with the heavier log drops back, runners on the front-running team with the lighter log drop off to help the other team. Then, as the team with the lighter log starts to fall behind because so many men are on the other one, women from the surrounding audience offer their shoulders and the likelihood is that the two teams end in a dead heat. Such games, played without compromise, are not races in the sense most people think of them in dominant cultures.

After describing a Xavante log race in which he participated, in his book, *Millennium: Tribal Wisdom and the Tribal World,* David Maybury-Lewis writes, "It was a ceremony, an aesthetic event. They were as nonplussed by notions of winning and losing as we might be if a Xanvate turned to us at the ballet, after watching the principal dancers lead athletically off the stage, and asked 'Who won?'" (152) He goes on to explain that the event links the realm of Nature with the realm of human culture. The purpose of the ceremony is to stress that the dynamic tension between opposing principles need not tear the world apart.

There are many other ways to develop courage and fearlessness besides games. I close with some things to keep in mind in all of life's experience. (Some of these guidelines for living life in ways to develop more courage come from annotated recommendations I offered nearly two decades ago that still are true today.) *Primal Awareness: A True Story of Survival, Awakening and Transformation with the Raramuri Shamans of Mexico.*[7] They take into consideration four considerations about learning to become courageous and fearless. The first is to avoid the absolutism of duality with the courage to seek complementarity in apparent opposites. The second is to embrace mystery and a willingness to admit you do not know for certain, and that is OK. The third is to fully comprehend the power of fear to make you hyper-suggestible to perceived authority figures and their words. And the fourth is to consider that courage is about being, doing, thinking, believing, and acting in ways that helps us be more virtuous. The goal is for us all to become like the Indigenous People who still remember the original instructions. As Paul Nash writes in *Authority and Freedom in Education,* we can become like "original men who allowed themselves to be aware of complexity and contradiction and sought to integrate them into an even more complex whole by replacing fear with creativity" (253).

- The next time you feel fear or anxiety, identify it and list as many positive possibilities that might result from it.
- Whatever we continue to affirm can become a reality. Fear is generally more about our historical affirmations than it is about the uniqueness of the situation.

- After the initial fear response, if it continues in any way take a moment to analyze the words you use and evaluate the degree of their accuracy.
- Consider how the current fear relates to other fears. Make the connection and evaluate whether or not and to what degree the earlier fear is coloring the new one and make authentic adjustments cognitively and in trance.
- Find how you are positively connected to what is responsible or seems responsible for the fear or anxiety. What aspects of it or its source have a complement for your own well being?
- Investigate as to whether any sense of guilt is associated with the fear and know the difference between artificial and preventive guilt. (Primitive guilt is illustrated by a lion that kills a rabbit even though he is not hungry. The lion remembers this incident and the memory only if it is about to happen again and the memory prevents it and is again dismissed. Artificial guilt occurs if the lion would say to himself continually after the first mistake, "Oh what a bad lion I am.")
- Sometimes when fear relates to ego death we can allow it to die while use TBL to imagine a rebirthing.
- Use every fear or anxiety as a conscious opportunity for practicing a virtue.
- Use courage to be truthful in describing the things that make you unwilling to engage them and be sure to recognize when some old fear is responsible. If it is, use trance-based learning to re-envision a different form of engagement and "go for it."
- If materialism and convenience become too captivating, force yourself into an experience of relative discomfort and simplicity in nature and learn to recognize that which you fear or are unduly uncomfortable with. Your own vision question is an option.

Another way of looking at becoming courageous and fearless is to become the author of your own life story. This does not mean your story is not interconnected with other stories, but that in the end your life is guided by honest reflection on lived experience and is not dependent upon external authorities. This seems easy to say and maybe to do, but it is not the way of our dominant worldview, as the next chapter reveals.

Notes

1. In the AAOS 8th edition on page viii they write, "Be careful what you say at the scene of an emergency because words, even when spoken in jest, can become fixed in the patient's mind and cause untold harm." In the 10th edition,

this was watered down significantly to simply say "Words can hurt a patient so be careful with them." It seems the number of people who referred to the original quote, as I did in my text Patient Communication, made too much of it being related to fear-based spontaneous hypnosis. AAOS was responsible for changing Jones and Bartlett from republishing my text because they felt telling someone to stop their bleeding is "going to far." (Recall this book, published by Brady-Prentice-Hall, was remaindered shortly after publication owing to fear of litigation.)

2. Although I do not advise the reader to intentionally create fearful situations to stimulate spontaneous hypnosis, I have done so often when I worked as a professional hypnotherapist and sports psychologist. A humorous and perhaps more radical example happened a few years back when I was helping fencing champion Nathalie Moellhausen get into the Olympics. We were in Cuba for the international trials and the night before her final competition, she began to worry excessively upon learning her first draw was an especially intimidating opponent. As I was thinking about this I was looking out my sixth floor window of our old hotel and she was waiting for me next door in her father's room for a hypnosis session I opened the window, side-stepped along the ledge and knocked on the window. Nathalie heard the tap first and looked up toward the window. When she saw me she screamed. Her speechless father opened the window and I nonchalantly invited her outside for the session. Of course, we did not need to go outside and the rest is history (See Self Magazine).

3. When I first wrote, "weak sister," I was not thinking about a number of Indigenous stories I had read like the MicMac story of "The Invisible One." (See http://www.firstpeople.us/FP-Html-Legends/TheInvisibleOne-Micmac.html). This and other American Indian stories like it is a classic Cinderella story except instead of beauty that wins a high placed marriage, it is courage. The cruel sisters with less courage were ultimately the weak ones.

4. According to his student Plato, "he was the best of those who lived at the time" (Phaedo 118), but unlike Spinoza who came along more than a thousand years later but remembered little of the original instructions. Spinoza's contention that everything in the universe is One and can be conceived us as Nature which is a manifestation of God (Stokes 79). Of course, as a result, he "remains the lesser studied and least regarded of the philosophers. He was excommunicated from the Jewish community for his views, denounced as an atheist by Christians, and declared so wicked that at one time his books were publicly burned.

5. The term "indigenous knowledge" denotes the traditional understanding of a community which has originated, grown and lived in a specific area (WIPO 2001, 23). Indigenous knowledge is therefore 'naturally possessed' by a particular community, and its content may be as broad as human experience: from history, to astronomy, biology, health and agriculture. The process of validation of this form of knowledge involves its use and usefulness in the real world (Bhola 2002, 11). Unlike western science, which is knowledge about how to live, indigenous knowledge is a way of life: it is the actual living of that life (Johnson 1992; Nakashima 1993).

6. Gandhi also believed there were two essential worldviews, the dominant one and the original one, and he was forthright about not supporting the dominant one. According to Ghandian scholar, Dr. Anuradaha Veeravalli, Gandhi's choice is clear: "The question for him is a matter of the distinction between modern civilization and true civilization, not between modernity and tradition"(Veeravalli 18). He quotes from Gandhi's writing in his 1939 publication, *Harijan*, "The democracies, therefore, that we see at work in England, America and France are only so called because they are no less based on violence than Nazi Germany, Fascist Italy or even Soviet Russia. The only difference is that the violence of the last three is much better organized than that of the three democratic powers" (Veeravalli).

7. *Primal Awareness* was about my coming to first realize the relationships I describe more deeply in this book that came to me after a near-death experience.

3

Community Oriented Self-Authorship

The wind, the trees, the animals, the corn, our friends, our suffering,
our dreams-only these things tell us what is most important. Everything shows itself
through our experience. Corruption comes when we pay too much attention
to someone else's experience.

—Augustin Ramos, Raramuri

Native Americans have some of the most eccentric people in their communities because
it is recognized the individual takes into consideration and acts upon the needs of the
community and does not act on the basis of selfish interests alone.

—Lawrence W. Gross (251)

Knowing the power of intentional and unintentional trance-based learn-ing and how the latter can make us susceptible to believing untow-ard communication from authority figures, we can understand one reason self-authorship is important in the Indigenous worldview. When we are in control of our thinking and trust our intuitive insights our natural trance awareness helps prevent misdirection from external influences. It gives us the authority for what we can then instill in our minds to achieve. If some-one such as a trusted shaman or psychologist has certain skills at hypnosis, we might tentatively authorize him or her to help us form the most effective images, but we do so with full awareness.

More important than avoiding negative influences from perceived authority figures however is that self-authorship via Indigenous worldview gives high degrees of individual autonomy to people while at the same time assuring that people use their freedoms to help their communities. In Indigenous worldview, the highest authority for all decisions comes from one's personal, honest reflection on lived experience with the understanding that everything is related. It is this understanding that makes a distinction between self-authorship as it is generally perceived in the dominant worldview and that of the Indigenous one. Self-authorship is always ultimately in the service of the greater good in the latter.

Self-authorship in Indigenous ways of thinking comes from knowing that the highest authority for decisions comes from honest reflection on lived experience in light of realizing that everything is related in life and this interconnectedness must be a part of all decisions. Michael Anthony Hart, aka *Kaskitémahikan*, gets to these ideas about inner authority coming from such reflection:

> Through inward exploration tapping into creative forces that run through all life, individuals come to subjectively experience a sense of wholeness. This exploration is an experience in context, where the context is the self in connection with happenings, and the findings from such experience is knowledge. *Happenings may be facilitated through rituals or ceremonies that incorporate dreaming, visioning, meditation, and prayer.* (Italics mine) The findings from such experiences are encoded in community praxis as a way of synthesizing knowledge derived from introspection. Hence, Indigenous peoples' cultures recognize and affirm the spiritual through practical applications of inner-space discoveries. (Hart 4)

Such a holistic understanding of accessing, trusting, and exercising our inner authority is the source of the creativity and knowledge synthesis we need for addressing our global problems.

Willie Ermine refers to this inner authority with the Cree term *mamatowisin*, which is "the capacity to tap the creative life forces of the inner space by the use of all the faculties that constitute our being–it is to exercise inwardness" (Ermine 104).

This understanding is missing from our dominant worldview where objectively based outward exploration is sought for guidance rather than introspective knowledge development. Dependence on external authority is the rule in spite of the call to question authority that has always resonated on the fringes. Under the dominant worldview obedience trumps community oriented self-authorship. Decision-making is rarely a holistic process or does it utilize alternative states of awareness, deep reflection and community praxis. The random quotations below[1] selected from an Internet search reveal that obedience to authority is common under dominant worldview:

- Obedience to lawful authority is the foundation of manly character. (Robert E. Lee)
- All religions have based morality on obedience. (Alexander Herzen)
- Obedience brings peace in decision making. (James E. Faust)
- Justice is the insurance which we have on our lives and property. Obedience is the premium which we pay for it. (William Penn)
- I was not born to be free—I was born to adore and obey. (C. S. Lewis)
- Every game has rules. Life's a game that has its respective rules; obey the rules, win the game! (Israel Ayivor)
- A wolf cannot have more than one head or it tears itself apart. (Conn Iggulden)

From a social dissident on the fringe:

- Any dictator would admire the uniformity and obedience of the U.S. media. (Noam Chomsky)

From an Indigenous raised Dakota:

- The American Indian was an individualist in religion as in war. (Ohiyesa)

Reliance on external authorization is not only the bedrock of choices in mainstream society and the main approach to moral development but it also guides jurisprudence and conflict resolution. Authorized punishment or revenge is a primary goal for wrongdoing. Under Indigenous worldview, bringing offenders back into community via affected members of the community is the goal. This relational approach expands the circle of bland and seeks input from a wide circle of relevant people. Spiritual resources are employed via prayer or song and subjectivity is as important as objectivity. Hart emphasizes this relationship as emphasizing "spirit and spirituality and, in turn, a sense of communitism and respectful individualism" (Hart 3).[2]

In the Indigenous worldview, communitism refers all of our relations and not just the human ones. It recognizes that "all things exist according to the principle of survival . . . and have a role to perform to ensure balance and harmony and the overall well-being of life" (McKenzie and Morrissette (259). To survive requires a deep appreciation for diversity and its role in helping us learn the many facets of truth that support surviving and thriving. Actual and symbolic wisdom from other-than-human sources are often more important than that which comes from the humans.[3] Notice how the idea of community oriented self-authorship supports and is supported by seven principles of Indigenous worldview offered by Leanne Simpson, whose *Nishaabeg* name is *Betaasamosake* and who directs the Indigenous Environmental Studies at Trent University in Ontario:

> First, knowledge is holistic, cyclic, and dependent upon relationships and connections to living and non-living beings and entities. Second, there are many truths, and these truths are dependent upon individual experiences. Third, everything is alive. Fourth, all things are equal. Fifth, the land is sacred. Sixth, the relationship between people and the spiritual world is important. Seventh, human beings are least important in the world.[4]

Without guidance from other-than-human life that surrounds us, humans make many mistakes (in spite of Socrates' claims that he could learn only from other humans in towns and not amidst trees). Thinking errors certainly abound today with our dependence on external authorities to guide us. A number of books have been written with some embarrassing statistics about this, like *Just How Stupid Are We?* (Shenkman) and *The Dumbest Generation: How the Digital Age Stupifies Young Americans* by Mark Bauerlein. Shenkman writes about widespread susceptibility to meaningless phrases, stereotypes, irrational biases, and simplistic diagnoses and solutions that play on our hopes and fears. This speaks directly to our focus on trance-based learning, the need for courage and the problems relating to dependence on external authority. Bauerlein also blames a lack of self-authorship: "Ignorance is not merely the lack of knowledge, but self-destructive turning away from truth in all areas of life. Persons develop a taste for ignorance, the predisposition to embrace erroneous beliefs based on presumption or mere authority. The ignorant person believes he knows what he actually doesn't know; he becomes delusional" (20).

Shenkman and Bauerlein's texts focus on United States citizens, but the citizens of other countries are equally "ignorant" in similarly dangerous ways. For just a few many examples:

- A 2006 study in behalf of a campaign called WildAid to save sharks found that 75% of Chinese were unaware that shark fin soup came from sharks (the dish is called "fish wing soup" in Mandarin) while 19% believed the fins grew back and very few understood the impact on shark populations.
- Exxon and most other oil companies knew of climate change in 1981 but funded deniers for 27 more years and continue to do so. As a result of this and the media that feeds such corporate sponsored falsehoods to the receptive public, in 2015, 56 percent of the 114th U.S. Congress questioned the 97% of scientists who support what a number of us see with our naked eye and intuitive insight—that a devastating human-caused change in climate is occurring.
- The large number of people who remain ignorant about the historical and current facts regarding Israeli occupation and settlement development in Palestine, with much of the ignorance funded by externally authorized beliefs from Christian evangelists.[5]
- Unawareness of the ecological implications of world trade agreements like the existing North American Free Trade Agreement and the currently proposed Trans-Pacific Partnership
- The acceptance of official stories and the growing fear of "conspiracy theorist" pejorative labeling to question them as relates to everything from 9/11 and the Iraq war rationale to US support for the dirty wars against the Indigenous Peoples of Guatemala.
- In spite of published studies regarding the loss of global biodiversity and the fact that the majority of researchers believe a human caused premature mass extinction is underway, most people are either unaware of this probability or choose "to turn away" from the reality.

This list could go on to include many other areas of concern that relate to our collective survival. The blame for such unawareness, ignorance, or apathy fundamentally rests with our tendency to trust and/or obey uninvestigated information or declarations from perceived external authorities. Of course, the institutions we have created that encourage this overdependence are also important to consider. The most important one is the education system, for it destroys the natural self-authority with which we enter the world all too quickly.

Education and Community Oriented Self-Authorship

My favorite true story about how Western education has long missed the mark as relates to teaching that which can help us survive relates to an event that took place in the early English colonies of Virginia and Maryland. (This was over a hundred years before U.S. and Canadian governments recruited Christian missionaries to forcefully abduct American Indians and Canadian Aboriginals from their families and placed them in residential boarding schools where they suffered cruel assimilationist practices and many died.) On June 17, 1744, commissioners from the colonies negotiated a treaty with the Natives of the Six Nations at Lancaster, Pennsylvania. As part of the deal, they were invited to send some of their sons to William and Mary College. After thinking it over carefully and discussing the gracious offer in council, the following response was sent to the commissioners:

> We know that you highly esteem the kind of learning taught in those Colleges, and that the Maintenance of our young Men, while with you, would be very expensive to you. We are convinced that you mean to do us good by your proposal; and we thank you heartily. But you, who are wise, must know that different Nations have different Conceptions of things and you will therefore not take it amiss, if our Ideas of this kind of Education happen not to be the same as yours. We have had some Experience of it. Several of our young People were formerly brought up at the Colleges of the Northern Provinces: they were instructed in all your Sciences; but, when they came back to us, they were bad Runners, ignorant of every means of living in the woods . . . neither fit for Hunters, Warriors, nor Counsellors, they were totally good for nothing. We are, however, not the less oblig'd by your kind offer, tho' we decline accepting it; and, to show our grateful Sense of it, if the Gentlemen of Virginia will send us a Dozen of their Sons, we will take care of their Education, instruct them in all we know, and make Men of them. (Cited in Reyhner and Eder 21)

The educational priorities of the well-intended commissioners like most state funded education today has always been about maintaining the status quo for the ruling elite, whether or not it lends toward survival or greater good of the larger community. The commissioners, like most teachers and administrators, probably did not and do not fully realize this. Such is the nature of hegemony. Nonetheless, this is and always has been the ultimate goal for most educational policies.[6] I have written about such educational hegemony[7] elsewhere, as have many others. Here I want to suggest that the educational approach referred to as heutagogy may be the come the closest to supporting Indigenous approaches to learning as relates to cultivating community oriented self-authorship.

Heutagogy is similar to but should not be confused with self-directed learning which was promoted as a counter-cultural effort during the sixties. It was subject to the same dependence on external authority. "Heutagogy takes into account intuition and is based on action, reflection, context awareness, and the value of experience with others as integral parts within the learning process . . . looks to the future in which knowing how to learn will be a fundamental skill given the pace of innovation and the changing structure of communities and workplaces" (Kenyon and Hase 3).

Heutagogy thus engages the whole potentiality of human consciousness, cognitive, experiential, reflective, intuitive, metaphorical, mystical, and trance-induced. For millions of years we realized from our observations of life around us—our non-human teachers—that survival depended upon such a holistic way of being in the world. In the 1960s, large numbers of experiential observers at least temporarily came to question the validity of the cultural values of their times and began adding more or different dimensions of being to their lives. Scientists, students, philosophers, book writers, and citizens of the world seemed to awaken to the realization that status-quo socio-political systems were somehow threatening our very survival. Likely not conscious of Indigenous and dominant worldview influences per se, they nonetheless sensed this. Eventually, therefore, dependence on external authority still continued. As for survival skills, they remained relatively inauthentic.

One of the leading contemporary thinkers who recognized this problem and understood that survival is the first order for all of life was Erich Fromm. He may or may not have known that this premise was basic to Indigenous worldview per se, but he knew it was a natural instinct. In 1976, he wrote that we lost this instinct because of our dependence on leaders who took advantage of our sheepishness to lead us in self-serving directions:

> How is it possible that the strongest of all instincts, that for survival, seems to have ceased to motivate us. One of the most obvious explanations is that the leaders undertake many actions that make it possible for them to pretend they are doing something effective to avoid a catastrophe: endless conferences, resolutions, disarmament talks, all give the impression that the problems are recognized and something is being done to resolve them. Yet nothing of real importance happens; but both the leaders and the led anesthetize their consciences and their wish for survival by giving the appearance of knowing the road and marching in the right direction. (9)

I submit that it is possible because of our point of departure and how from it we have devolved to where a different set of values has taken hold that includes giving power to authorities that promulgate it. Egocentric concerns, indoctrination into reliance on external authority, pursuit of money, assumptions about human superiority, and a belief in guaranteed salvation have blinded us to basic survival principles. A loss of authentic and continual sense of humor might be added to this list. Humor may be the most obvious of all the Indigenous worldview manifestations I have witnessed. It is intrinsic to Indigenous trickster stories and to various clown symbols of the various tribal cultures. Humor maintains a constant balance between chaos and joyfulness.[8] Our reliance on external authorities to rationalize the continuation of such values and beliefs has made us delusional not in spite of our educational systems, but because of them.

Whole Brain Theory

The fragmented nature of departmentalized formal education also minimizes the potential of whole brain learning. As mere followers, we function with only a small part of our brain because without community oriented self-authorship we are always worried something will be taken away from us by those in control of things. Amidst worries about survival, our susceptibility to simplifying our task by putting ourselves in the hands of authority figures is a natural inclination when community oriented self-authorship is not a life mandate. Any system of being or education that fully embraces human consciousness, cognitive, experiential, reflective, intuitive, metaphorical, mystical, and trance-based learning requires whole brain engagement.

This idea that worry (stress, fear, anxiety, etc) does not only minimize our self-authorization potential by causing unnecessary and often harmful reliance on others, it also reduces our full capacity for mental processes according to neuroscience.[9] A strong commitment to conceiving and sharing the humor that can somehow mitigate the stress in concert with courageous community oriented self-authorship would therefore reduce worry and expand brain involvement. According to Jeffrey Fannin and Rob Williams:[10]

> This information is mostly subconscious. Worry disrupts the "brain-bridge" (corpus callosum), sand slows the transfer time from the left to the right hemisphere, taking additional time for processing without creating a solution to the problem. Leaders or managers who are constantly worried often see this worry as an attempt to find a solution, but may in fact be stuck in worry, which usually keeps productivity to a minimum. The Whole-Brain State increases communication between the left and right hemispheres of the brain, and speeds up the transfer of information across the corpus callosum, thereby diminishing the capacity to worry. (15)

Thus it seems that whole brain activity is ultimately about complementarity (a later chapter), and the corpus callosum provides a synthesizing location for collaboration between right and left hemispheres.[11] This was also revealed in a remarkable study by one of my doctoral students research studies. Interestingly, it manifests not in the whole brain physically but in the corpus callosum. An experiment I briefly mentioned in a previous note that was conducted by one of my doctoral students for her doctoral dissertation hemisphere function and the tranquility effect of Nature reveals how whole brain activity is enhanced by a reduction in worry. The dissertation author, Joo-Yeon (Christina) Ri, correlated nostril dominance and brain hemisphere activity by taking brain photos of participants watching two films while in an MRI machine. Using the largest and most state-of-the-art MRI machine in the world, located at a medical university in South Korea, Joo-Yeon had subjects watch portions of Al Gore's alarming documentary, "An Inconvenient Truth," on global warming while brain activity was recorded. Then the subjects watched a simple "sights and sounds" of nature film Joo-Yeon had produced, depicting natural, pleasant, everyday images of healthy natural environments and creatures. During the watching of Gore's documentary, high levels of brain activity revealed deep cognitive thinking. The hypothalamus and pituitary centers stimulated the release of stress hormones while watching and listening to the dire predictions of what might happen if we do not take effective action soon. However, when the simple nature film was watched, cognitive functions were largely absent. Visual and auditory functions were minimal. This calming was accompanied by activity in the fibers communicating between the right and left hemispheres via the corpus callosum, indicating not only a relative lack of stress but also a healthy balance between left and right brain (Ri).

If we consider the stress of loss of autonomy or of being obedient in ways that go against one's values, we can see how community oriented self-authorship can increase whole brain activity. Combine this with the fact that "most of our daily decisions, actions, emotions, and behavior depends on 95 percent of our brain activity that goes beyond our conscious awareness" (Szegedy-Maszak 59) and that community oriented self-authorship coupled with fearlessness and trance-based learning can enhance conscious awareness and you can see why these three Indigenous worldview precepts (trance-based learning, fear management, and community oriented self-authorship) are so important for creating solutions to our world problems. We cannot do it with only 5% of our brain functioning!

Egalitarian Chiefdoms and Self-Authority

Like the claims I have supported relating to Indigenous worldview approaches to trance use and fear management, I argue that community oriented self-authorship indeed guided and guides most societies living in accordance with our Indigenous worldview. Like prevalence of warfare or degrees of health, controversy about whether Indigenous Peoples were more or less hierarchical continues. Anti-Indian perspectives often bring forth images of authoritarian hierarchy in the same way they promote Indigenous cultures as war-mongering, superstitious savages.[12] However, in contrast to dominant worldview systems, such as that of the European models, a strong case can be made to show that not only were most Indigenous cultures not hierarchical but even when they *were* community oriented self-authorship still was a strong worldview assumption that was implemented. Keep in mind that my point-of-departure theory relates to a time when agriculture hoarding and surplus came about and not just because of farming. We now know that early gatherer-hunter societies practiced agriculture and animal husbandry to some degree.[13] In any case, most American Indian social structures were:

- nonhierarchical
- matrilineal
- egalitarian
- classless
- gender balanced
- without single authoritarian "chiefs"
- based on generosity and greater good ethics
- guided by distributed leadership
- individualistic and supportive of the community at the same time

Peter Gray, in his piece "How Hunter-Gatherers Maintained Their Egalitarian Ways" writes that the hunger-gatherer version of equality meant that each person was equally entitled to food and group decisions were made by consensus. "One anthropologist after another has been amazed by the degree of equality, individual autonomy, indulgent treatment of children, cooperation and sharing in the hunter-gatherer culture that he or she studied." He offers three complementary theories behind the ability to maintain such systems of egalitarianism and I have added a fourth:

1. Reverse Dominance Hierarchy. Even when hierarchical leadership emerged owing to charismatic leadership or authorized management of scarce resources, the people would not tolerate anyone trying to lord over others. Ridicule, teasing, and, in extreme situations, ostracizing of anyone showing a sense of superiority cultivates cultures of humility and authentic equality
2. Emphasis on Humor and Playfulness
3. Permissive Childrearing
4. The belief that the non-human entities that surround us are the teachers and we the students. When we learn that we are not su-

perior to frogs or fish or grasshoppers or corn or invisible spirits, it is hard to feel superior to another human no matter how different they may seem. Thus I contend that the dominant worldview's anthropocentrism is an important reason rigid and abusive hierarchies that have existed for thousands of years under dominant worldviews.[14]

Probably the best evidence for asserting that egalitarian behavior originally described all pre-point-of-departure human societies comes from studies of Aboriginal social structures. Traditional Aboriginal societies lack political centralization and have complex systems for such behaviors in accordance with supportive worldviews. However, a number of Indigenous cultures did have strong hierarchies at least just prior to Western invasions. Because they still practiced these four beliefs/practices, for the most part the hierarchies maintain large-scale egalitarianism far beyond the hierarchical structures of the world under dominant worldview. In spite of archeology and paleontology researchers who describe ancient Hawaiian, Mayan, or Aztec cultures as having brutal caste systems with absolute rulers, such realities of hierarchy cannot be determined from the material record in light of the Western lens through which researchers understand hierarchy. In *The Archeology of Rank*, Paul Wasson writes,

> Archaeologists cannot possibly observe the people they study, therefore must infer social rank from the material record. This also occurs when observing present societal actions—social hierarchy is not a tangible, visible phenomenon but rather something that must be inferred from observing individual actions. (44)

Similarly, Harvard trained anthropologist Christopher Boehm, Director of the Jane Goodall Research Center at the University of Southern California, and his colleagues extensively studied apparently hierarchal Indigenous cultures and came up with the theory of "reverse dominance hierarchy." They found that even when Indigenous cultures did have hierarchal social structures, they usually operated according to leaders of any kind being essentially dominated by the followers. In other words, a worldview that emphasized the morality of oneness or interconnectedness and greater good thinking caused a group's main political actors to assure that no one, not even an official leader, be allowed to truly dominate the group. The research on tribes with chiefdoms show that public opinion, elder councils, and the ideology of egalitarianism held the chiefs in check. Oral codes and spiritual egalitarian worldviews only allowed leaders to go so far with their advantages and rules. Authority for decisions may be given in certain hierarchical systems operating according to the Indigenous worldview, but coercive powers and anti-community mandates do not. Such leaders have been referred to as being "first among equals" whether he or she is a selected, a charismatic, or a hereditary leader. Boehm's extensive research and citations of many others whose work supports such conclusions. The bottom line is that under Indigenous worldview, "differences between individuals are only permitted insofar as they work for the common good" (Godelier 109).[15]

Although every society whether under Indigenous or dominant worldview has some ways of attempting to curb a leader's power, without self-authorship such a balance of powers, even if structured constitutionally as in a democracy, are weak. And if broad-reaching self-authorship is encouraged under Indigenous worldview and discouraged under the dominant one, we can see how the voice of the people has become either missing, ignored, or ignorant. Consider the work of Dr. Marcia Baxter-Magolda who found that self-authorship requires three elements to emerge and reflect on which worldview is most likely to cultivate them. First, she says that we must have an internal belief system that allows us to consider but not be overwhelmed by external influences. Second, we must have a strong, confident, courageous, and collaboration oriented self-identity. Third, we must be able to engage interdependent relations with diverse others. These she refers to as all being internal capacities (90). I suggest that what the reader has learned thus far would suggest that our Indigenous worldview is significantly more likely to create and cultivate such capacities.[16] Noting that her studies were about self-authorization and did not include a specific description of "community oriented self -authorization," I propose it would be even more likely to do so with the orientation.

In his 1997 publication *The Heat is On*, Ross Gelbspan prophetically warns that totalitarian Authority will soon replace democracy if we do not bring ourselves to solve the ecological catastrophes facing us such as global warming. He predicted that more and more climatic disasters will occur. He says more and more people will be forced to leave their homelands and settle elsewhere. This in turn will cause more authoritarian propaganda and mandates to control people and diminishing resources. All these things of course have happened with intensity during the past decade. By re-embracing our Indigenous worldview approach to community oriented self-authorization. This does not mean we should not listen carefully to others and consider the conclusions they have reached via their experiential reflection of course. Chief Golden Light Eagle's request for help with his dream is an example of how self-authorship and listening to others can work.

In a YouTube presentation several years ago called "The Chief's Dream," he asks the public for help with interpreting his dream about President Obama. Over the years he received nearly a thousand replies. A Lakota elder, he starts his presentation with the usual emphasis on self-authority by proclaiming that he is "Chief of nothing." He continues: "I don't lead anybody and I don't follow anybody except my spiritual grandfather and spiritual grandmother. We are just a piece of the puzzle, a part of the hoop. Try never to interpret your own dreams and you can make it into something that it is not." He then asked for help in interpreting his own dream. I paraphrase it below. I share it here because my own response has to do with the topic of this chapter.

> In the dream a crowd was following this man, a black man. It was President Obama. He told the chief he wanted to talk with him alone. The bodyguards opened a door to a white room with a white couch. The chief's feelings were a strong concern for Obama and he asked Obama how he was doing. Obama turned away as if the chief did not exist. He did not seem to be himself. He acted as if he was in jail and was looking how to get out. Then someone knocked on the door and the secret service people in black and white said that time was up. All the camera people came over and Obama started talking about how much he learned from the Native Americans and how wonderful his short time with the chief had been. He talked about all the things he would do for the Native Americans. The chief was perplexed and that is where the dream ended.

I could not help but respond to his request having been so personally disappointed in Obama's saying one thing and doing another. I close this subsection with my words in hopes that they can help remind us that whether or not we are in such powerful positions of authority, we all can find within our original worldview the understandings we need to do what is right in the world if we can find our courage and integrity once lost.

My interpretation of the dream is that the chief saw the truth about how to explain Obama's contradictions and his continuation of the Bush Doctrine. He cannot listen to any sincerity or truth, especially the holistic Indigenous truth of his Indigenous ancestors, for fear it will tear him apart. Not even in private, not even with the people of the time before deception. To do so would create a painful cognitive dissonance he could not resolve without dire consequences to him and his family. In spite of his charge, he had long ago lost his community oriented self-authorship or the courage to implement it. He cannot "be himself" as the Chief described the dream. On the one hand the power of his position is far too great and too dependent upon the great lie he knows he is living—too great for him reject it. On the other hand the weakness of his false power and his fear of consequences keeps him in his chains. In public he can only lie. To himself he must remain in complete denial. This is the plight of too many of us. Our superficial "power" (ego, wealth, control, etc.) has almost completely stopped our self-authorship and spirituality of oneness. And now we are in the throes of an unnecessary mass extinction, led by the tragedy of President Obama and other world leaders who remain in denial.

Regaining Community Oriented Self-Authorship

Once we stop searching for or responding to authority outside ourselves, we can begin to answer the question, "Who am I and what is my unique role in the universe?" We can respect our "guides on the sides" and listen carefully to their words without having to conform. No more reliance on the charisma of individuals, on "expertise," or official authority for right choices.

The following exercises can help assure the wisdom of our convictions and the courage to implement them and modify them when appropriate.

1. Choose any situation that you intuitively feel might be made better to bring you to a higher level of community oriented self-authorship. Then after reading the rest of the book, apply each of the interrelated Indigenous worldview beliefs (trance-based learning, constant courage leading to fearlessness, community oriented self-authorship, sacred use of words and art expression, and using Nature as the ultimate teacher) to your reflections on the way you are now. Use the CAT-FAWN metacognitive process to determine the source of authority for decisions and behaviors you make that seem to prevent you from your highest potentialities and contributions to the greater good. Each time you find that a major influence for your actions in the world coming from an external authority, investigate the truthfulness of the beliefs that came from it. Perhaps you can associate how you are now to an unintended trance-based learning event where a perceived authority figure's words stuck.
2. Use intentional trance-based learning to reconstruct the new way of self-authored interpretation that comes from honest reflection on lived experienced. Be sure to look at how authority relates to each of the targeted forces (in parenthesis above).
3. "Honest reflection on lived experience" requires a open-minded, critical analysis coupled with loving intuition and forgiveness for those who have misguided us. Fear of suffering similar consequences that were once suffered must not be a deciding factor if we desire true transformation. Self-hypnosis imagery reconstruct-

ing the original trauma so it has a different and positive outcome is useful as is imagining what can be. Remember that hypnosis is about believing deeply in the images for change.

4. Civil courage and resistance rather than fearfulness and apathy must underlie self-authorization. Speaking truth to power with a sense of respect and while seeking complementarity can inspire self-authorization in behalf of the world.

5. Replace the label of "expert" with "assistant" or "collaborator." Do not buy in to interpretations, diagnoses, or treatment declarations for solutions to problems from psychologists, lawyers, physicians, teachers, politicians, authors, parents, friends, or celebrities. More than ever before you have access to information on the Internet that, if used with reflection on experience, intuition, and trance-based meditation, can offer a more appropriate remedy most of the time. Eighty percent of the time we go to a doctor in the first place and follow his or her orders, it made no difference. Ten percent of the time it is helpful and maybe even life-saving. Ten percent of the time it will hurt or kill us. Self-authorization can play the odds with less of a gamble on chance (Carlson 44).

6. Self-authorization in behalf of the greater good requires constant awareness of our interconnectedness with all things as well as of knowing we cannot fully know the truth. Embracing mystery and practicing humility go hand and hand with self-authority. This does not mean playing small in the world for each of us expresses the same greatness as a soaring eagle, a giant tree or a heroic personality in some unique way.

7. Self-authorization is about having power and place. "Power is a living energy that inhabits and or composes the universe" and place is where we discover our true self (Deloria and Wildcat 141). Power often comes to us individually via animals or plants or some feature of place. This metaphysical sensibility is essential for authentic community oriented self-authorization. The Indigenous worldview is about relationship and self-authorization can only be authentic under it when it is ultimately about "all our relations."[17]

8. Find what you love, the true love that comes from helping others, and build your life around it whether it meets the expectations of others or not.

9. When in doubt, be content with the mystery and have patience until you are able to make a choice. Use this book's Medicine Wheel to find out if a dominant worldview belief is holding you back and substitute it with the Indigenous worldview and employ your trance-based learning whether through meditation or self-hypnosis.

10. Remember in the Indigenous worldview truth is a multifaceted, moving target that can be known in degrees but seldom articulated. This does not make it "relative" but complex enough to call on humility and humor.
11. Pay heed to how external authority figures can use language in ways to evoke new beliefs when we are in spontaneous trance that makes us hyper suggestible.

Notes

1. Quotations are from http://www.goodreads.com/quotes/tag/obey and http://www.brainyquote.com/quotes/keywords/obedience.html
2. "Respectful individualism is a way of being where an individual enjoys great freedom in self-expression because it is recognized by the society that individuals take into consideration and act on the needs of the community as opposed to acting on self-interest alone" (Gross 129).
3. Leanne Simpson, whose *Nishaabeg* name is *Betaasamosake* and is Director of Indigenous Environmental Studies at Trent University in Ontario, has offered seven principles of Indigenous worldviews (2000): First, knowledge is holistic, cyclic, and dependent upon relationships and connections to living and non-living beings and entities. Second, there are many truths, and these truths are dependent upon individual experiences. Third, everything is alive. Fourth, all things are equal. Fifth, the land is sacred. Sixth, the relationship between people and the spiritual world is important. Seventh, human beings are least important in the world." I believe it more accurate to describe her second precept as a different perspective on truth rather than a different truth. This subtle difference in language is important, however, for Indigenous worldview harbors neither individualistic relativism nor communitarian relativism. It does assume a universality of "truth" that is manifested in the complex systems of cooperation in Nature but only that it is so mysterious and complex that it requires ongoing observation and diverse perspectives to come close enough to know how best to live while never knowing it so well as to claim an absolute.
4. I believe it more accurate to describe her second precept as a different perspective on truth rather than a different truth. This subtle difference in language is important, however, for Indigenous worldview harbors neither individualistic relativism nor communitarian relativism. It does assume a universality of "truth" that is manifested in the complex systems of cooperation in Nature but only that it is so mysterious and complex that it requires ongoing observation and diverse perspectives to come close enough to know how best to live while never knowing it so well as to claim an absolute.
5. An interesting dissertation explains "the overlapping histories of colonialism and nationalism, land struggle, as well as second-class citizenship, which manifests in exclusion, discrimination, racism and oppression of Mayans and Palestinians in the states of Mexico and Israel, respectively, are the grounds for comparison" (Eqeiq). When I was in Palestine, a woman in a bombed out shelter responded to my question, "What will you do?" by saying, "I only know we do

not want to wind up like your Red People who are forced into concentration camps called reservations."

6. See Noam Chomsky's presentation, "What are Schools For?" on the web.

7. My text *Teaching Truly: A Curriculum to Indigenize Mainstream Education* looks at seven subject areas in schools and before showing how to weave in an Indigenous worldview teaching perspective it identifies how corporate and other hegemonic influences shape curriculum, pedagogy, and textbook choice.

8. I suggest reading the excellent book about Indigenous humor by Kenneth Lincoln entitled *Indi'n Humor: Bicultural Play in Native America.*

9. Although I hesitate to put too much credibility into neuroscience because of the potential for its interpretations to be strongly influenced by the dominant worldview (Four Arrows, Cajete, and Lee), it still has a complementary role in helping us understand and reclaim our original worldview as long as we are aware of the potential problem.

10. These two authors are involved with a particular business that uses a variety of approaches, some scientifically based and some not, to enhance rapid belief changes, so I use their journal article with some reticence owing to the potential conflict of interest and a lack of more supporting data from independent research. I trust in it, however, because of my student's dissertation work which came to similar conclusions.

11. David Levine, a brilliant innovator, Sun Dancer, and CEO of a large solar company, referring to right and left hemisphere activities as "solar-lunar" balancing, writes about this bridge that holistically organizes complementary information, calling it "the step beyond versatility (context switching between solar/control and lunar/experience) is integration! This is the expanding the bridge for free-flowing information" (Personal email).

12. See for example the exposure of such poor anti-Indian scholarship in the text that sets the record straight about the Yanomami. Salamone, F. A. (1997). *The Yanomami and Their Interpreters: Fierce People or Fierce Interpreters?* Lanham, Maryland: University Press of America.

13. Recent research calls for a reconsideration of "hunter-gatherers" because it is revealing that they did more gathering than hunting and because they were also engaged in various degrees of agriculture and domestication of species. See pages 115–116 in Nancy J. Turner's *Ancient Pathways, Ancestral Knowledge: Ethnobotany and Ecological Wisdom of Indigenous Peoples of Northwestern North America,* Volume 1., 2014. Montreal, CA: McGill-Queen University Press.

14. See my family's peer-reviewed multi-generation authored article in UBC's journal, *Critical Education,* entitled "Anthropocentrism's Antidote: Rediscovering our Non-Human Teachers" (Four Arrows plus daughter and grandson).

15. Boehms cites French anthropologist, Maurice Godeliar, who was referring especially to the Baruya Natives of New Guinea.

16. In spite of the corporate oligarchy that has taken it over, the founding systems of governance articulated in the constitution of the United States is a remarkable model for egalitarian rule based on community oriented self authorship. It is also notable that the founding fathers of the United States, most notably Thomas Jefferson and Ben Franklin, consciously modeled it on the Iroquois Confederacy. Seldom taught in American schools and with contin-

ued scholarly rebuttals, there were no models in Europe at that time for what was created. For more on this see Bruce E. Johansen's "Adventures in Denial: Ideological Resistance to the Idea that the Iroquois Helped Shape American Democracy" in (Four Arrows) *Unlearning the Language of Conquest.*

17. *Mitakuye Oyasin* is a common prayerful phrase use when going in and out of an inipi (Purification lodge) and means "All my Relations."

4

Sacred Communication

In the Native ethic, "Communication" becomes a bond or covenant
between earth and humans. There is no value in communication unless
it is sacred and a blessing to the land.

—Thomas W. Cooper (98)

Bringing these worldview issues to the forefront of consciousness,
rather than having them influence us only subconsciously, is one way to add new
perspectives to some of our most vexing cultural problems.

— Dan Moonhawk Alford ("Manifesting Worldviews in Language")

In this chapter, I describe elements relating to the third direction of our medicine wheel. The sacred power of language is discussed in order to facilitate self-reflection and transformation. I describe how we can use Indigenous worldview concepts about words, songs, art, drumming, ceremony, visioning, telepathy, and other forms of communication[1] to better understand and express the complexities of reality, create new realities, share experiences, and maintain relationships with the natural world. In concert with the phenomenon of hypnotic learning and dominant structures of authority, language is instrumental in guiding our beliefs. Thus, I propose that Indo-European

Point of Departure, pages 91–116
Copyright © 2016 by Information Age Publishing
All rights of reproduction in any form reserved.

languages, especially English, were developed in order to reflect and support the dominant worldview. Each language contains its own wonders and usefulness and can be used more holistically connected to Nature if we employ intentionality and creativity. Those of us who do not speak an Indigenous language fluently can learn to employ sacred communicative expressions using the language we speak,[2] reconnecting us with the spiritual elements of place. We also can foster greater respect and responsibility for Nature.

Indigenous "Languaging"[3] and Landscape Ecology (A Theoretical History)

Although there is much debate about the connections between language and culture, discussions about the relationship between language, grammar, syntax, and landscape are largely absent.[4] Of course, traditional Indigenous knowledge clearly asserts that language was created to sustain our direct relationships with nature. "Each language is a link with the particular landscape in which a people live" (Peat 224). In *Power and Place*, Vine Deloria, Jr. and Daniel R. Wildcat write, "Because the world we inhabit is a very diverse place, we ought to understand what nearly all American Indian worldviews readily acknowledge: cultural diversity is not an issue of political correctness but is a geographic, historical and biological reality" (37).

Such importance given to Indigenous languages accentuates the tragedy of their loss and continuing disappearance.[5] I submit that there is a clear link between Indigenous language extinction and species extinction. It is no coincidence that the relatively small portion of Earth containing most of the world's remaining biodiversity is held by Indigenous Peoples. In "The Role of Indigenous Peoples in Biodiversity Conservation (The Natural but Often Forgotten Partners)" the World Bank's senior biodiversity specialist, Claudia Sobrevila, writes:

> Traditional Indigenous Territories encompass up to 22 percent of the world's land surface and they coincide[6] with areas that hold 80 percent of the planet's biodiversity. Also, the greatest diversity of indigenous groups coincides with the world's largest tropical forest wilderness areas in the Americas (including Amazon), Africa, and Asia, and 11 percent of world forest lands are legally owned by Indigenous Peoples and communities. (xi)

In spite of Indigenous claims about the inherent relationship between original languages, spirituality, and landscape, I have found almost no Western scientific research on the dynamic relationship between Indigenous languages and geography or landscape. Nonetheless, it seems obvious that

Indigenous languages reflect a kinship with place and its flora, fauna, and spiritual energies. For example, British Columbia has the most diverse landscapes in Canada, with rocky coastlines, forests, lakes, rivers, grassy plains, inland deserts, and snow capped mountains. Is it coincidental that in spite of comprising only ten percent of Canada's total landmass, it is the most linguistically diverse region of the country, with more than 30 Indigenous languages still spoken there? Of the 11 Indigenous language families throughout Canada, eight are spoken in British Columbia (University of British Columbia). Similarly, South Africa has the most diverse landscape in Africa, and the most languages of any African country, with 11 officially in use. In South America, Columbia has more language isolates (languages with no known historical or linguistic relationship to any other languages) in Africa (Bench 282). It also has more tree diversity than in the African equatorial forests. Are these coincidences, or are the Indigenous perspectives correct?

If Indigenous languages relate more to landscape, the languages that emerged post point of departure should be structurally different in ways that might reveal this. There would also be as much difference between Indo-European and Indigenous languages as there is between the two worldviews. Indeed, this seems to be the case. Indigenous languages emphasize process, subjectivity, transformation, and living connections with a more verb-oriented structure. One who closely observes nature realizes the constant transformations in landscapes. Indo-European languages emphasize categories, objectivity, permanence, and a separation from nature with a more noun-oriented syntax. A highly regarded theory about the history of the Indo-European language origins could support this claim.

Recall my story about the original point of departure in the Introduction: "This transition to a concentration of power eventually culminated in a phenomenon of social transformation when the Akkadians created history's first empire in Northern Mesopotamia (near modern day Syria/Turkey/Iraq) around seven to nine thousand years ago." If this is true, one might expect a change in language supporting the new worldview that began to separate humans from nature. Indeed, this may be the case. Recently, it has been theorized that the Indo-European languages originated at about this time and in this location. Published in the journal *Nature*, this theory is called the "Anatolian farming hypotheses." It claims that Indo-European languages—half of the languages in use today—expanded with the spread of agriculture from Anatolia approximately 8,000–9,500 years ago (Gray and Atkinson 435–439). The astonishing proliferation of these languages arose largely from violent territorial incursions such as the Roman and Norman conquests.[7] These conquests were a natural progression from the post point-of-departure hierarchal structures, and the increasing emphasis on anthropocentrism, greed, technology, and warfare.[8] Whether or not the reader accepts this theory, I describe how we can be more mindful about thinking and communicating in English in order to minimize the potential for unconsciously demeaning other-than-human life and categorizing or dividing all life forms into fragments.

An Academic Controversy

In order to understand the possibilities for speaking English more intentionally with flux and flow, I begin with an introduction to the long-standing academic debate about whether language is related to worldview, culture, or landscape. I believe that it does, and that we can use Indigenous worldview and communication approaches to improve our language syntax and use the power of words and other forms of communication to more authentically describe reality, enhance relational ethics, reduce deception, and manage unconscious thoughts and behaviors. However, some people believe that these issues have nothing to do with language, but are only related to other cognitive abilities.[9] In any case, one position tends to support the ideas of the late Benjamin Lee Whorf; the other relates to MIT linguist and social dissident, Noam Chomsky.[10]

Whorf's essential position is that language shapes worldview. He tends to believe that the structure of a language constrains the thinking of people using that language, and shapes their beliefs. Chomsky's position is that language is biologically universal for humans, like being given an arm instead of a wing, and that it is separate from other cognitive capabilities such as thinking. He believes that there is no compelling evidence to support Whorf's ideas.

Most Indigenous educators and language specialists whom I know generally agree with Whorf's ideas. In essence, I think both he and Chomsky have some valid conclusions and much common ground open to yet unproven possibilities. What follows is an overview of their different positions,[11] and my ideas about them. I offer these concepts in order to overcome some of the difficulties that impede optimal communication on behalf of peaceful, sustainable environments. My discussion about what Whorf or Chomsky "see," "say," "think," or "believe" comes from my own interpretations over the years.[12]

1. Chomsky understands language as a unique capability of humans, and does not consider non-human communication to be language per se. I disagree, and believe that we have unique linguistic and cognitive capabilities, while other creatures also have their own unique languaging. Whorf would likely agree with my position.

2. Chomsky believes that the function of language is not communication, and says that biological systems don't have functions. Whorf sees language as a form of communication, as do I. The complexities of human language incorporate more than the universal similarities in syntax such as those that relate consciousness, thinking, epigenetics, and intentionality.

3. I agree with Chomsky that language is one of several cognitive capabilities, but I also agree with Whorf that it cannot be separated easily from other capabilities. I think the overlap between language and other capabilities is too complex for the kind of empiricism he demands.

4. I agree with Whorf that humans develop language from, and for, their environment and relationships. As far as I know, neither Whorf nor Chomsky has considered my theory about the two major language groups, and how Indigenous languages relate to one kind of environment, while the Indo-European languages relate to another.

5. Chomsky believes in a "universal grammar" for all humans. Whorf believes that grammar is significantly different when comparing Indigenous and dominant language groups. I agree with both in that there is a universal structure relating to the use of sentences inherent in the human brain. However, this structure can be influenced by other things that can change grammar structure significantly enough to determine very different beliefs.

6. Neither Whorf nor Chomsky has written about or discussed trance-based learning or hypnosis in connection with language and communication. However, Chomsky once agreed in an email with my statement that I thought a group of people had been "hypnotized." Chomsky is known for his work about "manufacturing consent" and the ability of media to influence people. However, he has clearly dismissed Skinnerian behaviorism, and the idea that social control is a dominant phenomenon. I see Chomsky's position about media influence on social control as one of several contradictions, in addition to his writings that dismiss the 9/11 truth movement. While Chomsky states that syntax is basically common in all languages, I think there are basic similarities and significant differences that reveal his position as overly simplistic.

7. Chomsky's position is that language merely provides a vehicle for expressing thoughts produced by deeper levels of the brain. Whorf would probably say that language produces the thoughts. I posit that both positions are true and scientists have no way to prove either one conclusively. However, I lean toward Whorf's position that we think in relationship to the words and meanings we know.

8. Chomsky does not believe that language evolves; Whorf does. I agree with Whorf.

9. Chomsky believes that linguistic study requires a biological context, and must employ traditional scientific practice. Whorf understands that more subjective observations are important and useful. I have already seen how neuroscience and technology are influenced by language and worldview, so I strongly disagree with Chomsky on this point.

10. Chomsky asserts, "All work on the evolution of language is on the wrong track because it is about evolution of communication not language" (Rieber). Whorf and I disagree. (I believe that my arguments earlier in this chapter have not been studied by Chomsky or Whorf, and await a response from Chomsky following an email I sent to him yesterday.)

11. Chomsky believes that language cannot tell us anything about psychological reality or biological nature. I quote John Lucy's interpretation of Whorf in his book about Whorf's theory: "Ultimately, these shaping forces affect not only everyday habitual thought but also more sophisticated philosophical and scientific activity" (471). I agree with Whorf as interpreted by Lucy.

12. In an interview with Chomsky, Rieber questions whether the Navaho and Hopi have different structural qualities centered on the verb rather than the noun as a function of the environment. Chomsky replies, "True, those languages differ from, say, English, in many different respects. What differences there may be are obviously environmental. That is, I don't say the sentence in Navaho, and the Navaho doesn't say the sentence in English, but I assume that there is no relevant distinction in genotype. We obey the same principles of universal grammar." Notes by "environmental," Chomsky only refer to the fact that we learn the language(s) that surrounds us. He is not referring to the notion that the landscape creates the differences. Chomsky adds that he knows of nothing substantive that would support another theory at this point.

In summary, I agree with Chomsky that there are some universal, innate structures relating to human language, but others also are developed. I also agree with his obvious observation that we speak the language others are speaking when we are in certain surroundings. I disagree with him and agree with Whorf's idea that our language significantly influences how we think. Something neither of them seem to address, however, is my contention that the original development of language came from choosing words, sounds, and syntax in ways that helped to describe that which seemed important to the particular worldview. Thus, Indigenous languages related to landscape and all of interconnected life in the visible and invisible world. Indo-European languages that emerged post point of departure were more aligned with human-centered hierarchy, materialistic power, competition, and technologies for profit and convenience. Both language groups were created from worldviews and proceeded to build upon, rationalize, and maintain those worldviews while representing a wide variety of local, cultural, and spiritual beliefs. This does not mean that languages other than the Indigenous cannot be used in accordance with our original priorities, only that we must work a little harder when using them to ensure that we are avoiding a continuation of status-quo hierarchy, materialism, competition, and selfishness.

Incorporating Indigenous Worldview into Dominant Languages (and Other Forms of Communication)

Essentially, "working harder" to incorporate Indigenous worldview into our English language communications means to be more consistently aware of our words as they relate to the following concepts. By becoming more aware of the Indigenous worldview, we can significantly rebalance our relationships with all life forms. This increased awareness can enable educators in all disciplines to teach students:[13]

1. The power of words
2. Emphasis on movement and respect
3. Truthfulness
4. Decolonization
5. Telepathy
6. Creative expression

The Power of Words

In a speech for the Royal College of Surgeons in London in 1923, Rudyard Kipling shared one of his most quoted passages:

> I am, by calling, a dealer in words; and words are, of course, the most powerful drug used by mankind. Not only do words infect, egotise, narcotize and paralyse, but they enter into and colour the minutest cells of the brain, very much as madder mixed with a stag's food at the Zoo colours the browth of its antlers. (n.p.)

Recall my reference in Chapter One regarding the controversial text I wrote about how most medical emergency patients are in spontaneous hypnosis during the first hour of trauma. Although Kipling never mentions hypnosis, I have often wondered how many of the surgeons listening to these words actually understood the connection. This speech was given long after James Braid became famous for using hypnosis in surgery, and two years before Josef Breuer died the same. One might think that the connection would have been made between Kipling's speech and the power of hypnosis in medical practice. If today's attitudes are considered, I suppose they did not make the connection.

The same problem exists for all of us living under the dominant worldview. Words are tossed about without realizing their great hypnotic power, except when used persuasively, often regardless of the truth. Words can contradict reality, or freeze it. They can limit our options when our mind is in a trance. When a salesperson asks, "Do you want to sign the contract with my pen or yours," if you are in a light trance induced by his images of what you would like to buy but cannot afford, you will fall into the trap that stops you from saying, "No thank you."[14]

According to educational linguist Matthew C. Bronson, "The first lesson may seem obvious, but is worth restating in more modern terms: '*all words hypnotize to some extent, that is their function.*'. . . Moreover, the sacred lessons embedded in native languages can point us toward an ancient, more sustainable and human future." A wide variety of traditional Indigenous cultures understood the intrinsic power of words. They knew that a word embodied as much force as a river or lightening. They believed that words activated and/or influenced not only other humans, but anything to which they referred in the visible and invisible worlds that comprised reality. This is why the Raramuri and other tribal peoples would not mention their hunting prey's name before or during the hunt, except when engaging in very carefully orchestrated ceremonies asking the prey to give its life to the community. Words have such power because they are active participants in defining and understanding reality.

This brief discussion of the power of words might lead you to assume that everything you say is a potential hypnotic directive, including self-talk. If you have more adipose or fatty tissue on your body than you consider optimal and say the words "I am fat" when you look in the mirror, you may be hypnotizing yourself. Moreover, the sentence "I am fat" is not accurate or truthful, and being truthful is the most important quality for "right languaging." Similarly, how we discuss the world creates social realities that may continue or reverse the sixth mass extinction.

Emphasizing Movement and Respect

The example about saying "I am fat" would be less likely to occur if we used Indigenous worldview and language construction to guide how we use English sentences. Such absolute, categorical, and permanent declaratives would not exist. How would thinking and communicating be different if we attempted to use language to emphasize action, experience, and the potential for becoming? What if we tried to minimize any form of "to be," instead saying "I am" or "he is?" For example, "I am regularly teaching." "He is acting badly now." This Indigenous worldview orientation on motion and temporariness counters the tendency to make things more permanent as occurs with the ease of labeling and categorizing the English language affords. This could help us imagine changing things to address our global crises better. If language can emphasize transformative learning instead of status-quo thinking, it might help us discover more creative ways to address climate change and other causes of mass extinction.

In linguistics, language that emphasizes movement is referred to as "manifesting versus static," "reality-oriented," or "process-based." The most common reference to such languages seems to be "verb- or noun-oriented." Indo-European languages are predominantly verb-oriented, especially English. "It is widely known that the number of nouns is larger than that of verbs in English children's early vocabulary" (Gentner). Shore found 80% nouns and 20% verbs in English-speaking children under the age of four. Children also show a preference for nouns. In fact, most Indo-European languages emphasize subjects and objects. Japanese, often considered a verb-based language, is also "essentially noun oriented," although nouns clarify the relationship between and a complement in English and the described event itself in Japanese.

Indigenous languages are mainly verb-oriented. For example, the structural grammar of Indigenous languages is almost completely based on verbs. English words we think of as nouns function more like verbs. For example, "man" is thought of as an act of doing that which a man might do. A rare example of an English phrase that turns nouns into verbs is in the sentence, "It is raining." The "it" is thrown in because the language structure virtually demands it. In a verb language, "raining" describes a movement. Although a few Indo-European languages omit the noun "it," it is an exception, whereas most Indigenous languages do this with most nouns. For example, in Lakota where verbs are the most important linguistic element with more than 500,000 verb forms listed in the Ethnos Project's Online Lakota Dictionary, *magazu* is a complete sentence that can be translated as "it is raining" or "there was rain." Without the English perspective in translation, the meaning considers the movement and a variety of nuances, depending on the kind of rain and the place where rain falls. In Lakota, even a house is not a noun, but more like the word "*tipi*" which reflects ideas about "living in." By adding small particles called affixes, such nuances are described; in effect, these are like adverbs instead of adjectives. So "a good horse" would be "horse doing goodly" (*Sunkawakan kin waste*). Young and Morgan, as well as Gentner and Boroditsky offer similar evidence in their study of the Navajo language. For example, they found that Navajo verb morphology is more productive than its noun morphology, with approximately 6,245 nouns compared to 9,000 verb bases (analogous to English infinitives). The nouns were largely formed from verbs.

Does it really make sense to consider aligning English communication with the worldview wisdom that developed Indigenous verb-based languages? I believe it does, as do others. According to Dr. Bronson, When we contrast indigenous and western languages and worldviews, we can begin to reclaim aspects of the old language that undergird both. In "Lessons in the Old Language," he answers the question, "What if god were a verb?" with a reference to the writings of Algonquin elder Dan Moonhawk Alford.

> What if god were a verb, an unfolding dynamic processing? Perhaps it would be harder to fight and kill as so many have done in the name of "god" if the Native view were more widely held. Verbal thinking is complementary, dynamic and contextual, rather than dichotomous, static and universal. Problem situations and people are much harder to categorize as "things" that one must confront and destroy in a verbal-based reasoning with fully animate subjects. (Alford)

Indeed, the concept of god is a verb in most Indigenous languages. For example, in Lakota, *Wakan Tanka* god is literally the "great mysteriousing." While we cannot know the details about the creative energy of the cosmos, the idea of continual manifestation offers a respectful, engaging way to conceive of such a force.

In fact, the movement orientation of Indigenous languages makes almost everything potentially animate, including rocks, trees, carvings, and just about anything else, depending on one's perceptions and relationships. On the other hand, our grammar of dominance makes it too easy to polarize nouns into "this or that," or "us and them." This allows for double-bind hypnotic language easily persuading us to unconsciously choose one side or the other without considering many other options. And then there is the problem with the inanimate "it" pronoun which demeans what we have been taught to conceive as inanimate. "It is a whale." "It is a river." How are we going to protect such "things" when we think of them in this way? If we do not know whether a newborn baby is a girl or a boy, do we really feel comfortable referring to the child as "it?"

I close this section with words from Leroy Little Bear on this topic regarding the importance of a movement or transforming languaging:

> In my language, Blackfoot, the point to be made is that I don't think we can underestimate this process-action base of the language....There is something behind the word. There's a spirit, a power, some energy behind it,...The circle is never closed, because this spirit that's behind it could manifest itself as something else too. (159)

The take-away I intend for this section is to practice and experiment with making language represent a combination of precise truthfulness coupled with sufficient room for movement and change. For example, while walking on the beach with my wife, we were talking about Monsanto losing a court case with Indigenous beekeepers in Mexico. This led to discussing less successful outcomes. She said, "As long as people are greedy who control our corporations, we will be unsuccessful." I reframed it and said, "If those who are leading corporations continue to prioritize financial profiting more than joyful, healthful living, we can expect that our successful *transformings* will continue being blocked." Now this sentence is far from what we might be able to say in an Indigenous language, but by simply using as many action-oriented words as I could quickly think of and wanting to avoid concretizing assumptions or "us vs. them" perspectives, I think the second sentence is more constructive.[15] My wife said she felt more hopeful hearing the second version. I hope others will work on examples of how this practice can emerge and share them with me at djacobs@fielding.edu. De Villiers writes in "The Interface of Language and Theory of Mind" that false beliefs and understandings seem inextricably tied to certain language prerequisites.[16] It is past time to find creative ways of eliminating false beliefs that have dominated since our point of departure!

Truthfulness[17]

Knowing the power of language leads to taking great care in using it. The multifaceted nature of "truth" is best understood when we use process-oriented grammar that better reflects the ever-in-motion nature of reality. Accurate, honest language was vital for survival in the natural world marked by so many inherent risks. Today's convenient separation from nature may make us think that we are no longer facing such risks. In fact, we are creating much greater ones as the hurricanes, droughts, and fresh water depletions increase. Today, not only are we not careful in using language to describe reality, but it is common for people to intentionally use it deceptively. In *A Time before Deception,* Thomas W. Cooper explains that American Indians considered lying a sign of insanity. At first, they believed that the Europeans who consistently lied were unable to conceive of reality and needed to be pitied (Cooper 3). If lying and deception are a sign of insanity, then surely a communication or language that makes it more difficult to lie may be useful in healing this condition.

As we have seen, the Indigenous worldview-based languages are rooted in Nature. F. David Peat, a holistic physicist who lived among a number of Indigenous tribes, writes: "Words link man to the inner meaning of things. One sometimes gains the impression that deep within the hidden recesses of Indigenous languages the words of power can still be found that will enable people to communicate with the life around them" (227). Just like the non-human world teaches virtues such as courage, it also teaches truthfulness. Nature does not lie. Animals may have instinctive ways to hide food or stalk prey, but unlike humans, they do not misrepresent reality.[18] In the Indigenous worldview that honors individual autonomy as a way to work toward the greater good while respecting interconnectedness, valuing honesty reinforces the trust needed for survival and well-being.[19]

The reader may think that truthfulness is equally embraced under our dominant worldview. After all, from early childhood, most people are taught not to lie. We have been told over and over that we should tell the truth, but in reality, society and our dominant worldview encourage and reward lying. In his book *The Post-Truth Era: Dishonesty and Deception in Contemporary Life,* Ralph Keyes admits that we cannot prove people are lying more than ever, but he cites a number of studies, editorials, and anecdotes indicating deception is more prevalent and "the emotional valence of words associated with deception has declined" (13). Similarly, in the preface of her updated book on *Lying,* Sisesla Bok concludes that "we are all on the receiving end of a great many more lies than in the past" (xviii).

The assertion that lying and deception are founded in the dominant worldview is supported by references to ancient Greek philosophy and mythology. Lillian Eileen Doherty is the editor of Oxford University Press's book, *Homer's Odyssey,* that assembles 16 authoritative articles on Homer's *Odyssey.* This ancient Greek poem created near the end of the 8th century BC is considered the most influential work in shaping Western culture. It likely helped to shape the philosophy of Socrates, considered the father of Western philosophy. Through the epic story, deception, lying, and trickery are presented as admirable. Consider this passage from the translated document as the Goddess Athena transforms herself into a beautiful woman and speaks to the hero:

Any man-any god who met you would have to be some champion lying cheat to get past you for all-round craft and guile! You terrible man, foxy, ingenious, never tired of twists and tricks—so, not even here, on native soil, would you give up those wily tales that warm the cockles of your heart! Come, enough of this now. We're both old hands at the arts of intrigue. Here among mortal men you're far the best at tactics, spinning yarns, and I am famous among the gods for wisdom, cunning wiles, too. (Homer Book 13 lines 324–339)

Unlike Indigenous trickster stories designed to warn against being deceptive and untrustworthy, Homer's *Odyssey* accurately depicts early Greek civilization. J. P. Mahaffy, a noted Greek and Roman historian and author of seven volumes on Greek society, writes that dishonesty and distrust "was a feature congenital in the nation and indelible" (p. 46). According to classics professor Robert Littman, "The Greeks were obsessively concerned with the admiration and approval of their peers. This fostered a character who was vain, boastful, ambitious, envious and vindictive. Above all the arousal of envy and the obtaining of revenge were esteemed most highly" (18). Littman also explains that the function of lying in Greek society related to considering life as a struggle against nature and other human beings, a belief inherent in the dominant paradigm and absent in the Indigenous worldview. The Greeks considered the world to be hostile. This was especially true in peasant society where people were constantly on guard against thievery or worse.[20] He states that it was "commonplace to lie deliberately to children in an effort to get them to do something, and, while the child may become confused, never knowing whether an adult is telling the truth or deceiving him, he also learns what villagers regard as a crucial lesson, not to trust anybody, however close and dear, completely" (142).[21]

Another indication that deception is indirectly supported by the dominant worldview relates to how modern neuropsychologists see the world as revealed in their interpretations of scientific studies. When Indigenous scholar Greg Cajete, South Korean neuroscientist Jongmin Lee, and I attempted to show how brain science and neuropsychology supported ancient Indigenous wisdom, we were surprised to learn that many studies contradicted our theory. For example a number of these studies concluded that altruism was ultimately a selfish act intending that the generous act would beget a reward. Some contemporary neuroscience and neuroeconomics authors have shifted somewhat from this idea, showing that generosity is a more biological imperative than selfishness, and is more natural than competition. However, most researchers continue to interpret their experiments by saying that because acting in generous, altruistic, or cooperative ways activates a reward processing center in the brain, authentic generosity does not exist. We found that the use of artificial monetary rewards and punishments in laboratory experiments and the limitations of the most advanced technology filtered through the dominant worldview, and led to inaccurate conclusions about generosity and honesty. For example, in one study, Spence and colleagues concluded that "lying is a normal component of human social interaction."

In *A Time before Deception*, Cooper describes how he and an international team of scholars from 14 countries conducted over 200 interviews with Indigenous elders worldwide. They found that respect was a universal attitude guiding all types of communication. After analyzing hundreds of codes of ethics to which Western communication professionals aspire, they found that respect was seldom mentioned. Freedom, responsibility, and truthfulness were often cited, but interviews of journalists, public relations staff, and entertainers revealed that most of them believed that such values were not consistently applied. I contend that the lack of respect for other than humans supported by the dominant worldview is the foundation for disrespect among humans and the practice of deception, especially related to the pitfalls of capitalism.[22]

The take-away here is to realize that it is more difficult to be honest and/or accurate with the English language, and that we can use Indigenous worldview and its communicative orientations to better use English and other dominant language families with conscious awareness and increased effort ensuring that words come as close to representing truth and accuracy as possible, especially during intentional or spontaneous trance states.

Decolonization

Language domination is a major vehicle for ideological hegemony. That the English language is the most dominant colonizing language today, and is responsible for the murder of more Indigenous languages than any other, is undisputable. Linguistic and ethno-cultural diversity are nearly as important as biodiversity and support its well-being. There is a correlation between loss of cultural identity worldwide, the incursion of English, and species extinction. According to the Indigenous worldview, language diversity far outweighs the benefits of having a common universal language. In fact, language diversity is so important to Indigenous Peoples that the Arawak tribes in Northwest Amazonia in Brazil and Columbia consider marrying someone who belongs to the same language group akin to incest (See Alexadra Aikhenval's chapter in Camacho et al., *Information Structure in Indigenous Languages of the Americas.*)

In spite of the debates between Chomsky and Whorf about the relationship between language and culture, I propose that European languages facilitate colonization and neoliberal globalization. They make it easier to categorize, objectify, and concretize realities than those that emphasize movement, change, complementarity, and diversity. Ideological hegemony stems from language dominance and structures that make hegemonic assumptions more transferable.[23] For example, one feature of many Indigenous languages of the Americas that might help to explain how Indigenous English makes it easier to create or sustain antagonist or competitive relationships relates to "evidentiality."

Evidential orientations are linguistic structures that indicate the evidence of a claim. This generally includes whether what is said comes from visual, auditory, or hearsay sources (Comacho 4). To better understand experience and truth, such devices are important for communicating within a worldview that highly respects subjective knowledge, the importance of diverse versions of experiencing similar situations, and consistent accuracy in describing reality. Primal languages are developed with such structure to help keep the event being described open to diverse perspectives that enhance the true understanding of reality. For example, our eyes might tell us that the moon is larger when it is on the horizon and smaller when it is overhead. In English, we might tell someone, "Look how big the moon is." This could confirm the illusion semantically. A child overhearing the parent making this statement could believe the sentence literally. Various Indigenous languages would have many descriptors built into words that would convey a more accurate utterance. In English, we might say "Look, my eyes are showing me this moment while the sun is fading in the direction of the west, that the moon is showing itself bigger." To replicate this linguistic device in English would require extra intentionality and awareness. The English language does not embed such structural grammar to easily allow this feature to emerge, but as the example illustrates, it is something we can all do if we are aware of the power of language.

Another example of how most Indo-European languages, especially English, might be more useful tools for language dominance and hegemonic colonizing relates to the wide-ranging word structures for predicates, including non-verbal ones. In other words, the part of a sentence that tells what a subject does or describes something about the subject has great flexibility (Comacho 11). Imagine the different reaction someone might have when hearing "He lied to me," opposed to "In offering a perspective from his own frightening experience, he spoke of his own wishing about how things could have been thus being incomplete in describing." Using polysynthetic phrasing, an Indigenous language might say this with one word.[24]

I offer four take-aways for how we can use English in a more decolonizing way. The first is to be conscious of the problems facing Indigenous peoples everywhere, and support them whenever possible. This includes efforts to save Indigenous languages. The second is to carefully listen to, or read sentences with an attitude of critical thinking. Study the meaning of educational, ideological, and cultural hegemony, and how easily it is to fall for them.[25] The third take-away is to start using language in ways that help you and those with whom you communicate make words ring true, and keep the different worldview considerations offered in this chapter in mind as they relate to language and other forms of communication. The fourth is to tell stories often as a way to convey ideas or information. Storytelling has long been used for decolonization by Indigenous storytellers. Honor Ford-Smith (1987) asserts that, "The tale-telling tradition contains what is most poetically true about our struggles. The tales are one place where the most subversive elements of our history can be safely lodged..." (p. 3). It is not a coincidence that many decolonizing efforts of Indigenous Peoples involve forms of communication created and fostered by musicians, artists, and storytellers.

Telepathy

With telepathic communication, we *might* have less concern about linguistic structures such as grammar and syntax.[26] I do not know if my telepathic experiences were diminished or enhanced by thinking in English, or if what I conveyed and received was more manifesting or concretizing, but I assume it was the former. My work with wild horses certainly related to results and action. Some of the top "horse whisperers" have told me that in spite of their public descriptions about their techniques, they secretly believe that telepathy is at work, but they do not say this because people do not believe in it as much as when they refer to their technique with a name, like Feldenkrais.[27] Indeed, except for Rupert Sheldrake and a handful of other reputable scientists, most researchers do not explore telepathic studies because scientific journals will not publish them. Telepathy is categorized and dismissed as part of parapsychology.[28]

> The essential problem is that a large portion of the scientific community, including most research psychologists, regards parapsychology as a pseudo-science, due largely to its failure to move beyond null results in the way science usually does. Ordinarily, when experimental evidence fails repeatedly to support a hypothesis, that hypothesis is abandoned. Within parapsychology, however, more than a century of experimentation has failed even to

conclusively demonstrate the mere existence of paranormal phenomenon, yet parapsychologists continue to pursue that elusive goal. (Cordón 182)

Of course, the Western science dismissal of telepathic communication is not very different from its dismissal of Indigenous worldview precepts grounded in the spirit and the intelligence of Nature, which I believe telepathic communication to be. In *Native Science*, Greg Cajete explains: "The Western science view and method for exploring the world starts with a detached 'objective' view to create a factual blueprint, a map of the world. Yet, that blueprint is not the world. In its very design and methodology, Western science estranges direct human experience in favor of a detached view" (Cajete 24). In his book, *Synchronicity: The Bridge Between Matter and Mind*, David Peat does not specifically mention telepathy, but in discussing unexplainable communications between people, including dreams and visions, I believe he comes close to describing the phenomenon when he writes:

> We must also consider the limitations of our current worldview with its notions of causality, the arrow of time, objectivity, the separation of mind and matter, and the emphasis upon reproducibility rather than on unique, single events. Such events (as telepathic communication) may not be so much the result of a psychic link or mental communication but rather indicate that a mutual process is unfolding out of the same ground and that this ground must therefore lie beyond the individual consciousness that is located in space and time. (32)

In *Religions of the World*, Huston Smith found that primal people commonly used telepathy for communication. He describes the experiences of many people, and offers the possibility that telepathic communication continues in the dominant culture, but without the intentionality and controllable skills of traditional Indigenous Peoples. He tells about a time when he was visiting John Neihardt, the author of *Black Elk Speaks*. He says John and his wife were telling him about a minor automobile accident they were in, and their meeting with the insurance agent in their home shortly afterwards.

> The Neihardts had been sitting at the dining-room table explaining the accident to the agent when he interrupted and said, "Would you mind putting your dog out? It's making me nervous."
>
> "Dog? What dog?" the Neihardts wanted to know. "Oh, you know. That little black spaniel." He glanced under the table and, seeing nothing, added, "He must have gone out." The Neihardts looked at each other in astonishment. They had had a black spaniel who had been the joy of their lives, but he had died of old age the week before.

After telling the story, Smith suggests that telepathy might have been the source of this phenomenon. However, I mention it here because Smith says telepathy is not a consideration in the dominant worldview.

> It does not require the conclusion that the spaniel's soul continued after he died and continued to impact the living, for it is equally possible that the insurance agent picked up telepathically on the Neihardts' remembrances of their dog. Still, telepathy too is not a part of the standard scientific worldview, so in either case the reported facts seem to challenge that view in one way or another. (Smith 219)

Telepathy is how I can best describe my experience with Raramuri shamans in Mexico. As I describe in my book, *Primal Awareness: A True Story of Survival, Transformation and Awakening with the Raramuri Shamans of Mexico,* Augustin Ramos explained to me how he brought a little girl out of a serious illness. Yet not a sound came from his mouth. So when I read about American Indian shamans, Tibetan psychic adepts, Achuar Indians of Ecuador, and Australian Aboriginals using telepathy regularly, I naturally believe it to be truthful, in spite of the lack of Western scientific support for this phenomenon. The shamans have told me that telepathy requires intense concentration on sending vibrational waves of thought by both sender and receiver, (this coincides with my work with wild horses described in Chapter One.) I believe we can rediscover and develop our telepathic abilities to talk with other "people" of any culture, and converse with animals, trees, and some rocks.

The take-aways here are to start practicing telepathic skills immediately. When listening to someone, concentrate carefully on intended meanings that may enhance, clarify, or make more whole what is spoken. Then ask questions to clarify what the speaker intended. The goal is to see what differences exist, and whether these differences confirm what you thought was intended. Another practice is to guess who is calling you on a phone before you know. When the telephone or cell phone rings, concentrate on who it might be and say what comes to you before you answer. Do this until you notice an increase in correct intuitive flashes and stay with it. Practice concentrating telepathically with your pets by giving commands without verbal or body language. With friends or students, there are many ways to practice telepathy. One is to place your hand on a magazine photo and have the friend concentrate on what it is while you describe what you "feel." Your skills will improve rapidly.

A powerful telepathic experience is when one uses it to communicate with Nature. Ask permission of a tree before you touch it and wait for a reply.[29] Notice carefully what you feel. I have been doing this exercise with children and adults for years, and am constantly amazed at the experiences even the most skeptical participants share afterwards. Perhaps this is what Herman Hesse did before he wrote "Trees are sanctuaries. Whoever knows how to speak to them, whoever knows how to listen to them, can learn the truth" (43). Finally, I suggest engaging in lots of "praying." By this English word, I do not mean the usual idea of asking some particular god to do you a special favor. Rather, I refer to entering into dialogue with the many spirit energies that surround you. Such praying is a form of telepathy similar to what happens in meditation, except in meditation, you are only the receiver of the telepathic communication. So pray with or through your thoughts, words, songs, or other modes of authentic expression by sending healing vibrations into the world on behalf of whatever relations come to mind.

Creative Expression

Most readers understand that dreams and visions play an important role in Indigenous art. Popular culture seems to have made the connection between dreams and visions. For example, many people know how images associated with Aboriginal Dreamtime influence the unique art of the Australian Aboriginal People. Art has long been a form of communication with our Indigenous ancestors. Every person was an artist who brought inner visioning to the surface in order to share with others via drama, music, painting, beading, sculpture, clothing, making tools, and so on. "All Tribal people engaged in the creation of artistically crafted forms . . . . Art was an integral expression of life, not something separate" (Cajete 149). There was no distinction between function, meaningfulness, and mastery of aesthetic expression. The dominant idea of art for art's sake or for entertainment,[30] profit, or egotistical recognition did not exist. Art was purposeful, communicative, useful, and meaningful for all who viewed it, regardless of whether viewers or users knew the artist. More educators are realizing that art was and is to Indigenous people, a major opportunity for communicating.[31]

Of course, to some degree, art also has served as a communication tool by those living in accord with the dominant worldview, although it is important to note that much communicative art has protested the cultural byproducts of the dominant worldview, such as anti-war or pro-union drama, songs, poetry, painting, and more. The arts have also been used to incite patriotism on behalf of war. In general, however, the widespread use of art that aligns with the dominant worldview as a communication phenomenon is marginal. In *Art as a Language for Communication and Critical Awareness (Or Not?)*, Anna M. Kinder from the University of British Columbia sees art historically as a constantly revolutionary form. She is not at all against its critique of culture, but the revolutionary qualities are not specific to anything outside the individual perspective. There are no common threads for an exchange of information, a prerequisite for communication. "Firstly, in my view, the statement that art, as it is practiced today, is a language that facilitates communication is significantly problematic" (Kinder 11). She adds that because art has become free from structures, rules, or conventions as would be necessary in a shared communicative language, it falls short. She believes that if art education could emphasize the ability to use art to express the experiences of everyday life (including dreams and visions), the ability to experience the world aesthetically could again be a very precious gift which significantly adds to the quality of life (Kinder 13). Ceremony has always been a foundation for traditional Indigenous arts.[32] Whether relating to experiences, dreaming, landscape, spiritual messaging, seasonal cycles, hunting, or courtship, spiritual harmony with nature is always the primary feature of authentic Indigenous art. The art we choose for transformative learning comes from that which connects us to the sacred. When we connect with creation through expressions that come from Nature, we make ourselves whole. We disperse the shadow of separateness that can loom over us when we over-affiliate with rational thought, entertainment, materialism, commodification, control, escape, activism, or any other endeavor wherein we lose touch with the spirit world that surrounds us. Art cannot stand apart from spirituality in our original worldview as when:

- playing the flute to communicate with, and court a lover while remembering the stories about its creation in the forest and its relationships with creatures .
- playing the drums with communicative intentionality[33] while remembering the pulse of the Earth.
- acting out a tragic drama, but recognizing how it may stir wisdom and emotions sufficiently to prevent a tragedy similar to the one depicted.
- telling a traditional story, realizing it came from the earth and can pass sacred wisdom on to future generations.

Making art based on this spiritual and transforming purpose allows for ambiguity and variety. Respect for process and materials, including their spiritual essence, certainly exists. Some artists become known for exceptional skill, but such recognition does not restrict anyone's engagement with the art form. Skills to ensure functional appropriateness can be a matter of survival. An arrow must be crafted to shoot straight and requires many hours of disciplined learning to select wood and feathers. Still, there is much room for individuality and creativity, depending on specific needs.

It is fine to show two legs of a rider on the same side of the horse in a painting. It is fine if someone else has an especially beautiful voice. This does not stop one's full participation. Everyone sings because the arts are a form of playfulness, stimulating us to try new ideas. As in play, humor abounds in all the arts, no matter how important art is for survival, or how tragic a story's message. In these ways, communicating via art offers a joyful, symbiotic relationship with others. I do not know if humor is a result of Indigenous worldview, but there is no question that Indigenous cultures use it far more often than the dominant culture. Because humor is often about taking a difficult situation and transforming it into something funny, some of the aforementioned ideas about Indigenous language seem to have bearing.

> The transformation of consciousness into a public form, which is what representation is designed to do, is a necessary condition for communication. What is clear is that culture depends upon these communications because communication patterns provide opportunities for members of a culture to grow. We develop, in part, by responding to the contributions of others, and in turn we provide others with material to which they respond. (Eisner 10)

Perhaps the symbiosis to which Eisner refers as a catalyst for transformation and growth points to a remarkable possibility, contrasting pre- and post-point-of-departure languages. What if they are intended to be complementary, and their murder over the past 8,000 years has been more suicide than genocide? There is a Hopi prophecy about a white and red brother who separated to different sides of the globe with different languages. One day, the two brothers reunite and learn each other's language. The result is a renewal of harmony on Earth. A theory by William K. Power in his book *Oglala Religion* is that Indigenous languages are essentially right-brained because their verb orientation emphasizes results rather than cause, and because time and space are inseparable. For example, a Lakota translation of "How far is it to Pine Ridge?" is "Letan Pine Ridge towhan hwo" which literally translates in English to "When is Pine Ridge from here?" According to Allen C. Ross, "Native American languages allow more right-brain expression, whereas European languages encourage almost solely left-brain expression.... After we learn each other's ways, we will become whole-brain thinkers" (Ross 57). Keeping this possibility in mind, and realizing that it is unlikely enough of us will learn Indigenous languages in time to reverse the conditions of our global crises, we can at least attempt to use our European languages in ways that utilize the aspects of Indigenous worldview we are studying.

The take-aways for using Indigenous worldview when participating actively in the creative arts include:

- Use trance states to inspire learning creativity and connectivity.
- Think of your art as creating vibrational frequencies to spread a particular message for the positive welfare of others throughout the cosmos.
- Use trance to find out what earlier hypnotically imposed belief has caused you to think you cannot sing, dance, or draw.
- Author your own choices about every aspect of your art.
- Set spiritual intentions throughout your artistic process. Whatever your religion, accept it as a way for you to resonate with making the world peaceful and ecologically healthy for all creatures, without the notion of exclusiveness.[34]
- Be aware of the kind of music or other art around you, knowing it can help to induce trance and influence beliefs if you are not fully aware. Many soldiers have marched into battle entranced by the sound of a trumpet and the intent of a drummer.
- Knowing music affects energy, note how different music makes you feel, and select the right times for the right music.
- Be courageous in choosing to become an artist.
- Share your art. Remember it is a form of communication, especially when it aligns with the precepts supported by the Indigenous worldview.
- Whatever art form, tools, intentions, or outcomes relate to your artistry, never stop using them to illuminate, integrate, and be inspired by Nature's physical and spiritual world.

This final guideline to connect to the natural world is important not only for the communicative expressions; it is about all things of importance in one way or another. The very idea of complementarity stems from Nature and its cooperative systems. Connecting to and abiding by "Nature" is our Medicine Wheel's fourth direction and this book's final chapter.

Notes

1. "Communication" is often considered in terms of one person wanting to convey information to another, but human languaging (the verb) represents more than this idea conveys. Expressions of language are not always about communicating information, but the idea of communication as some sort of exchange or reciprocity makes sense to me, so I continue to use the word.
2. Here I am mostly contrasting Indo-European languages, especially English, with Indigenous ones, as I explain later. As we learn to use our own language in accord with Indigenous worldview, I also intend that we respect the diversity of languages while doing everything we can to protect further loss of the Indig-

enous ones. I am not suggesting that such conscious awareness can replicate Indigenous languages or worldviews hewn from tens of thousands of years of observation and reflection. Part of the work in learning to implement what follows calls on giving full support in prayers and actions to keep our Indigenous languages alive and protect Indigenous Peoples and their unique cultural knowledge, sovereignty and homelands from continuing assaults.

3. The more we use verbs in our speech, even if we have to invent them, the more we can convey the idea that life is unfolding, changing, adaptable, moving and potentiating. So why not start with the concept put forth by the English word "language" so that the expressions of thoughts via words can be like life, emerging and ready for transformation, instead of frozen permanently and apparently unchangeably.

4. I refer to debates about social issues with bright and concerned academics and activists in which landscape and its other-than-human (and more than human) aspects are never mentioned.

5. This loss of Indigenous language and related knowledge is rapidly increasing worldwide. Linguists generally agree that half of the world's 6,909 languages listed by Ethnologue will be extinct within the next century. North America exemplifies the problem. About half of the languages are spoken now by only a small number of older people, and only eight are spoken by 10,000 or more (Lewis et al.).

6. I cannot help but wonder if the author or the editor selected the word "coincides," as it hints of minimizing the reasons, for this fact. The World Bank has long been an enemy of Indigenous rights and sovereignty. In 2014, it began a pro-Indigenous campaign. Whether it is authentic and sustainable or not remains to be seen in light of many continuing anti-Indigenous policies like carbon-trading, and I remain cautious.

7. Of course, the spread of the English language historically and today with globalization economics deserves mention, as does the continuing injustice stemming from the Catholic Church-supported "Doctrine of Discovery." For more see "UN Condemns Doctrine of Discovery" published in January, 2016 by the Romero Institute.

8. In addition to the website Peaceful Societies, a number of scholarly publications counter the "whitewashed" versions of history used in education and culture. See, for example, Douglas Fry's edited text, *Beyond War: The Human Potential for Peace* (Oxford University Press) and my edited book, *Unlearning the Language of Conquest* (University of Texas Press).

9. I refer to "academic" with the slightly pejorative definition of the word–learned ideas in higher education that have little useful significance. I say this with great respect for the intelligence, intentions, and intense scholarship of many people involved in the debate about whether and to what degree language and culture or perceptions of reality influence each other.

10. George Lakoff, Steven Pinker, and others in linguistics fields have weighed in with their own theories, but to keep from digressing too much into theory, using a brief overview of Whorf and Chomsky suffices. Although there are some serious disagreements on the surface that others have brought into the debate, an in-depth reading of Whorf and Chomsky would find that they agree

more than they disagree, and they are often misquoted. I do my best here to avoid doing similarly.

11. My overview is based on personal interpretations of their work and I may be incorrect. I do not intend, however, to take the time to cite or quote in an effort to support my view. I paraphrase some of Chomsky's words that can be found?? I draw from Chomsky's own words from a 1983 (Rieber) interview and a 2014 "Keio Linguistic Colloquium Syntax Session" on YouTube. Also of note is that I have been communicating with Chomsky for over a decade about a number of philosophical debates.

12. Interestingly, both of these key linguistic figures support the Indigenous worldview. Whorf spent much of his time studying the language of the Hopi and Navajo Indians and other Indigenous languages, and believed deeply in the idea that language and worldview were inseparable, and both were very different from the dominant worldview and its languages, even in terms of time and space.

    Chomsky sees no empirical evidence to support such an argument, but as his endorsement of *Teaching Truly; A Curriculum to Indigenize Mainstream Education* shows, he strongly believes in the worldview and knowledge of Indigenous People: "This enlightening book reminds us that the grim prognosis for life on this planet is the consequence of a few centuries of forgetting what traditional societies knew, and the surviving ones still recognize" (Back cover).

13. I wait for the day when an academic is permitted to write this way in scholarly texts. I did get away with this to some degree with my book, *The Authentic Dissertation: Alternative Ways of Knowing, Research and Representation,* by setting it up as a mock conference with invited scholars entering an imaginary dialogue with real dissertation authors, instead of citing their work. And other forms of arts-based scholarship are emerging. I also note that writing itself may be, in spite of its many advantages, more of a devolution (like many advanced technologies that have created imbalance). The complexity of orality and how it enhanced memory and forced a continuation of evolving truths was more useful than all the books of the world and the words frozen on dead trees (like this one).

14. This may be why most states have laws that give you three days to change your mind. In clinical hypnosis, the offer of only two options is a linguistic strategy known as an "either-or double-bind."

15. Although it may be harder to do this in writing than orally, in this book, I wish my English words could better express complementarity by not polarizing Indigenous and dominant worldviews.

16. Theory of Mind describes social-cognitive ability. See also the work of Astington and Jenkins, such as "A longitudinal study of the relation between language and theory-of-mind development" in *Developmental Psychology, 1999*(35), 1311–1320.

17. This is perhaps an ironic subheading, in that most Indigenous language did not have words for "being truthful;" doing otherwise was inconceivable.

18. Many observations of wild and zoo mammals have demonstrated the rescue and protection of other species with no conceivable self or species benefit. Researchers have begun to seriously consider this challenge to the survival of

the fittest notion, such as research published in "Why Are Animals Altruistic." *Science Daily*, 5 April 2006. Web.

19. It does not take much observation to see that communication between people today is not enriching the human spirit, fostering responsible citizenship, or preserving our commons. Anger, deception, ego defensiveness, lack of humility, materialistic goals at any cost, illogic, fallacy, absence of critical thinking dispositions, closed-mindedness, and the inability to argue honestly and cooperatively without trying to win plague interpersonal and professional communication, and precipitate the greed, inequity, and insanity that has brought us to the brink of extinction.

20. Robert Redfield, a noted anthropologist with the University of Chicago in the 1950s, wrote a number of books about peasant societies that maintained Indigenous worldview perspectives. He believed they represented values essential for returning modern civilization to a more non-violent, democratic disposition and moral order.

21. Today, it seems that such lessons continue with teenage lying at epidemic proportions and continuing into adulthood. According to the first internationally authored, cross-sectional lifespan investigation of deception, Debey and colleagues reveal interesting considerations related to the calamity of untruthfulness in dominant cultures. For example, lying behavior is influenced by the moral evaluation of lies, and lying reflects an increasingly positive evaluation of prosocial lies (55–56)

22. Walter Block, a colleague and co-author of our book on *Differing Worldviews in Higher Education*, writes "animals, birds, flora and fauna, etc. do not at all have intrinsic value, only instrumental value as a means toward our ends" (89). In our cooperative argument, Walter and I found some common ground, but this was not among them. Such a disrespectful belief may be necessary to rationalize economic externalities in free-market libertarianism, but it clearly has contributed to our being in the throes of a sixth mass extinction.

23. Consider how the phrase, "conspiracy theorist" has caught on to silence critical thinking about a number of issues, such as what actually happened on 9/11. My doctoral student, Ed Rankin, wrote a dissertation about this meme. His research reveals that its pejorative use originated with the CIA's intentional effort in the 1960s to stop speculations about John F. Kennedy's assassinations and continued to operate to challenge other anti-governmental speculations.

24. Polysynthetic languages allow the formation of extremely long and complex words created spontaneously out of many smaller parts.

25. My favorite example is how the story of Helen Keller is taught in schools, and how the majority of people from all walks of life who know she is a hero have no clue about why. If you are one of them, then this example is an opportunity for you to find out, as I would not want you to take my word for it. With Google, we still have the option to critically triangulate research questions in order to come close to what is and is not true. Without the skills to do this, Indigenous Peoples and all of us will have to fight against colonizing forces.

26. Since we likely think in terms of our language, syntax might play a role in telepathic communication; however, I believe that most messages one might attempt to send in this way would be so action-oriented that the images would

be more likely verb-oriented. Doctoral students might be interested in an Indigenous/mixed methods research project to explore this.

27. The famous horse trainer Linda Tellington Jones refers to her amazing work as "T-Touch," a form of the Feldenkrais method. But when a number of us specialized horse trainers spoke together, she told me (as did the other well-known people) that it was ultimately telepathy.

28. A recent (2014) telepathic experiment was, however, published in the "Peer Reviewed Library of Science" (PLOS One), so perhaps there is hope for Western science if telepathy proves profitable for the study sponsors. The team of distinguished researchers from Harvard Medical School, Axilum Robotics, and the Center for Noninvasive Brain Stimulation at Beth Israel Deaconness Medical Center "demonstrate the conscious transmission of information between human brains through the intact scalp and without intervention of motor or peripheral sensory systems."

29. It is not uncommon for Indigenous Peoples to speak to, and listen to rocks. "Not all of them talk," a shaman once told me. But be careful. The DSM manual the APA uses says talking to rocks and expecting a reply is a sign of insanity.

30. I am not saying that anything that is entertaining cannot be artful, but that art loses its communication power when entertainment is its only purpose. I love to entertain, but my love of it centers on the communication of playfulness via my "old time piano" playing and singing.

31. I am thinking of how it is used to help children communicate their identity and interests, but also how arts-based research has taken hold. See my text, *The Authentic Dissertation*, for example.

32. I know a number of Navajo, Seri, Tarahumara, and Lakota artists. I believe that they operate mostly from the Indigenous worldview. Due to the dominant world they must inhabit, some have lost the ceremonial part for the sake of efficiency. Sometimes this has caused a negative chain reaction, resulting in the loss of other important worldview precepts that have affected the communication aspect of their art. Others replace spiritual intentions with the profit motive and have lost their ancestral worldview.

33. See "Rethinking Indigenous Media: Rituals, 'Talking' Drums and Orality as Forms of Public Communication in Uganda" in the May, 2003 issue of the *Journal of African Cultural Studies* on the web.

34. I must be honest about my personal beliefs about religion. I think the founders of the major religions brought original teachings to their times, but under the dominant worldview, their primal ideas were quickly misappropriated and twisted into hegemonic devices. See my peer-reviewed study in UBC's *Journal of Critical Education* entitled, "False Doctrine and the Stifling of Indigenous Political Will." "False Doctrine" refers to a quote by Thomas Paine.

5

Nature as All

There were no temples or shrines among us save those of nature . . .
The tree, the waterfall, the grizzly bear, each is an embodied Force,
and as such an object of reverence.

—Charles A. Eastman (Ohiyesa)

Here is this vast, savage, howling mother of ours, Nature, lying all around,
with such beauty, and such affection for her children, as the leopard,
and yet we are so early weaned from her breast to society, to that culture
which is exclusively an interaction of man on man.

—Henry David Thoreau

We now face the fourth and last direction of our Medicine Wheel. Being mindful of the "Nature as All" aspect of Indigenous worldview relates to the other aspects of our wheel as follows:

1. We can best understand our relationship with Nature via trance-based learning because careful observations of plants, animals, insects, and landscapes require the use of trance-based learning

Point of Departure, pages 117–140
Copyright © 2016 by Information Age Publishing
All rights of reproduction in any form reserved.

      to fully communicate with them and to instill their lessons in our minds.

2. Courage and fearlessness can help end our alienation from the natural world while allowing us to practice virtuous relationships with others.

3. Self-authorization in concert with the other directions prevents us from being led away from recognizing our interconnectedness with all and leads us to more truthful realities.

4. Careful and honest communication that keeps landscape and other-than-humans in mind helps reduce categorization and hierarchy while allowing for transformational learning that brings us into closer harmony with Nature.

This chapter offers some Indigenous worldview precepts about our relationship to Nature that can help us implement these four possibilities.

There are a number of contemporary Indigenous scholars who certainly understand the relationship between Indigenous People and Nature, as I think I do. However, few if any of us speak from having lived fully outside the borders of the dominant cultures. Of course, there are Indigenous leaders and orators who do live in more traditional ways, like some leaders of the Achuar of Ecuador. Yet what they have written about in a few published works is mostly their battles against colonial encroachment into their territories. The majority also depend upon translators.

I could also cite the voices of early Indigenous people who lived traditionally and spoke orally to anthropologists and historians. However, I find the powerful truisms offered in relative short passages to be without the holistic context I seek for this chapter. Also, one cannot be sure of how much influence a sympathetic translator and writer had on the actual language. For example, consider this oft-cited speech by Chief Seattle:

> This we know. The earth does not belong to man. Man belongs to the earth. Whatever befalls the earth befalls the sons of the earth. Whatever happens to the beasts soon happens to man. If men spit upon the ground, they spit upon themselves. All things are connected like the blood that unites one family. Whatever befalls the earth befalls the sons of the earth. Man did not weave the web of life. He is merely a strand in it.

The version of this portion of his longer speech was written by a University of Texas professor and playwright named Ted Perry under contract with the Southern Baptist Radio and Television Commission, who edited and embellished the earlier version of William Arrowsmith, a literature professor at the University of Texas. Arrowsmith had edited the notes of Dr. Henry

Smith, who had created his version for the *Seattle Sunday Star* thirty years after the chief spoke his words in January of 1854 in his native tongue.[1] None
of this means to imply that the wisdom of the speech has been corrupted in
any negative way. I refer to it only to explain why I have chosen not to rely
upon such sources.

There are also a number of non-Indian People whose writing about human relationships with Nature conveys ideas about Nature that are similar
to mine and that are basic tenets of Indigenous worldview. I venture to say
that a number of these borrow from Indigenous worldview, whether from
the literature or from possessing it still in their DNA. Not the least of these
would be Henry David Thoreau. His philosophy stems from his intense
studies of the Indigenous perspective. In his text *Thoreau and the American
Indians,* Robert F. Sayre writes, "When Nathaniel Hawthorne met Henry
Thoreau in 1842, he noted that Emerson's young protégé seemed 'inclined
to lead a sort of Indian life among civilized men'" (Sayre xix). Indeed, Thoreau's major publications stemmed from 2,800 handwritten pages in his
"Indian Notebooks.[2] His goal was to write a book from these notes that
would help stifle the ignorance and anti-Indianism of his era, a book he
never managed to write. He also had the goal of learning the Indigenous
worldview. From Penobscot friends who lived nearby in the Maine woods,
he spent much time learning their language, a language he claimed was
"less artificial" and tended to reproduce the sounds of Nature (Sayre 122).[3]

I have chosen none of the above as my primary source of information
for this chapter. I have selected instead to present the published words of
Charles A. Eastman (aka Ohiyesa) and then to share my own insights and
ideas about implementation within our Medicine Wheel. Some may question my choice since Ohiyesa lived his adult life in the dominant culture
and became a Christian. Parts of his writing seem to reflect an assimilationist view as well. Nonetheless, I think his work is the best for my intentions
for the same reasons David Martinez states in his book *Dakota Philosopher:
Charles Eastman and American Indian Thought.* According to Martinez, a Gila
River Pima professor from the University of Arizona:

> Eastman demonstrates that the decision to embrace mainstream American
> life was not a simple choice between two evils—assimilation or extinction—
> but rather an arduous effort at maintaining core Dakota beliefs and prin-
> ciples in a radically different environment than the one in which Eastman's
> Dakota ancestors dwelled prior to westward expansion. Thus what makes
> Eastman a visionary or a "true philosopher" is his capacity to see through
> to the essence of things, whether it is being a Dakota or a Christian or the
> nature of modern life. (Martinez 6)

We all face a similar situation. We must consider our original worldview in an environment radically different from the one that produced it. Also, both Ohiyesa and I realize that although the social, political, and religious environment is different and the landscape is overwhelmed by the shadow of humanity, nature remains what it has always been, and it is important for us to remember how to live in harmony with it.

Thus, my goal here is to cite some Nature-related passages from Ohiyesa's book *The Soul of the Indian* and then to offer interpretations, along with some practical guidelines for a "Nature as All" worldview that may be used in conjunction with trance-based learning, courage, self-authorization, and an honest language that allows for movement. I begin with a brief overview of the author's life.

Ohiyesa's Background

Ohiyesa, meaning "winner" in Lakota/Dakota, was a Santee Dakota born in 1858 in Minnesota and raised by his full-blood paternal grandmother and an uncle after his mother died. In 1862 his family escaped the throes of the Dakota conflict by fleeing to Canada.[4] When he was fifteen, his father appeared as if from nowhere to bring his son back to Santee, South Dakota. A prisoner of the Dakota conflict, his father had converted to Christianity, taken the name Jacob Eastman, and been released to become a farmer in Santee, South Dakota. After working as a farmer for about a year, Ohiyesa was placed in the mission school at Santee, Nebraska. After two difficult years of forced assimilation, he was selected to go to Beloit College in Wisconsin and decided to go to medical school when he graduated. In 1887 he graduated from Dartmouth College and in 1890 received a doctoral degree from Boston University School of Medicine (Weiser).

His successful negotiation of Western education never really overshadowed his Indigenous view of life. He was the only physician to help the injured at the infamous Wounded Knee massacre. He worked tirelessly as an activist for Indian welfare, seeking a complementary rather than an assimilationist solution (Wilson). He was involved in establishing thirty-two Indian YMCA groups and helped the founders of the Boy Scouts of America and the Camp Fire Girls organize their priorities around living with and respecting Nature. He was the first person to write firsthand about the importance of Indigenous worldview. President Calvin Coolidge appointed him Indian inspector, and his recommendations were the basis of the Roosevelt administration's New Deal efforts to bring self-determination to Native Peoples.

As I mentioned, there are Native studies scholars, Indian and otherwise, who believe that Ohiyesa is not a good representative of Indigenous worldview. For example, in *Tribal Secrets*, Robert Allen Warrior refers to his work as misguided because it is more about assimilation by the dominant worldview than about a stand for the Indigenous one. In an article in the *American Indian Quarterly*, Drew Lopenzina sums up Warrior's description: "At best Eastman is considered misguided in his beliefs, at worst he is labeled a racist. But rarely does his life or work lend itself to an unqualified endorsement of his contributions to the movement of Native American advocacy" (Lopenzina 728). Lopenzina continues with his own perspective: "While acknowledging the problematic nature inherent in some of Eastman's stances, the author brings into greater relief his overall philosophy of a life of service—a philosophy he attributes to his 'wild Sioux upbringing'" (Lopenzina 729).

Martinez addresses Warrior's concerns, acknowledging that Ohiyesa did become a Christian, chose to get a non-Indian education, worked for the U.S. government, and so on. However, he believes Ohiyesa continued to speak from his Indigenous worldview. He mentions that Vine Deloria, Jr., often considered to be one of the most respected voices about Indianism in America,[5] had a high regard for Ohiyesa's work. He writes that although "Eastman is largely absent from Deloria's writings," when Deloria was asked by a graduate student to name his favorite books, "Without hesitation, Vine named *From the Deep Woods to Civilization* and *The Soul of the Indian*" (Deloria 7).

Another concern expressed by Warrior about Ohiyesa's writing has to do with its "pan-Indian" nature. Since, as I mention in the Introduction, my work in this book and in other publications also represents pan-Indianism, I do not see Ohiyesa's generalities about the commonalities in Indigenous worldview to be negative, any more than I feel are mine. Rather than regarding it as a step toward assimilation or loss of individual tribal identity, which admittedly is a risk, I see it as a way to bring more human beings into alignment with their own "tribal" cultures based on geographic localities and a return to a Nature-based life, which in turn can support the survival of the diverse Indigenous cultures and languages. I think that a focus on the primary and essential beliefs about Nature held in common by the great variety of Indigenous cultures may be a requirement for righting the boat in which we all are living and keeping it afloat.

To get a more complete picture of how Ohiyesa describes the Nature-based worldview he experienced as a youth and how he contrasted it carefully with the dominant culture in which he found himself immersed as an adult, I encourage you to read the entirety of his books. It might help to start with what Seneca scholar Barbara Mann refers to as Ohiyesa's "entertaining double voice" (Mann 33). Referring to his writing in *The Soul of the Indian,* she observes:

> For instance, most Westerners of 1911 would simply have glossed both "barbarian" and "savage" as indicating the Indians, but Eastman was cleverer than that.... A judicious look shows Eastman spending the first two pages of that chapter denigrating Christian practices as "artificial!" Next, Eastman immediately, and over the next score of pages, extols the moral beauties and rigors of the supposedly 'savage' Santee Sioux." (Mann 34)

Ohiyesa's Ideas on Indigenous Worldview as Relate to Nature

Regular Contact with Nature

Ohiyesa lived under the umbrella of traditional Dakota ways surrounded by Nature until he was put into residential boarding school. In spite of the pressures related to both forced and voluntary assimilation, he managed to hold on to his worldview to a significant degree. He wrote books because he wanted people to understand and regain intimacy with Nature while he suffered being deprived of its manifestations and vibrations in cities and towns. In his book *Indian Scout Craft and Lore,* he refers to the challenge now facing us all: "There are many deaf ears and blind eyes. Because the average boy in town has been deprived of close contact and intimacy with nature, what he has learned from books he soon forgets, or is unable to apply" (102). How can we face this challenge? What can people living amidst concrete and glass without the wealth required for sojourns into the wilderness do to re-engage with other-than-human energies? Among the many answers people offer are:

- The creation of more "Green Cities" by architects, engineers, and community planners with places where local citizens can go to be amidst trees and plants, along with the creatures they bring.
- A major shift in educational priorities that brings children out of classrooms and into areas where Nature can be embraced and seen as a teacher. Everyone, for example, can learn to communicate with trees. In a recent Sun Dance, my brothers and I spent two hours in dialogue with a single tree before cutting it down and decorating it for another four days of ceremony. During the two hours of learning about the tree and its wisdom, such as how its roots connected to other trees, how it had withstood a storm and its relationship with the bear whose claws had scarred it, all

of us were changed in some way and cried when we took our turns to chop it down and decorate it for the four-day ceremony.

- New approaches to valuing food sources that bring a connection to Nature, like creating one's own organic garden. In Cuba there are organic gardens on every block in the heart of impoverished cities. Why not in Detroit?
- Study of the sky, the stars, the sun and the moon in order to bring the Nature perspective to bear on one's personal and community life. Meditating while silently looking at them can evoke a Nature-based consciousness.
- When indoors, using art, music, and imagination in concert with trance-based learning to create metaphysical understandings about whatever it is you are doing. Making connections between all the tools and fixtures that surround you clarifies that the source is coming from Nature as a gift that requires responsible attention.

Now let's look at some suggestions for living life according to Indigenous worldview while living amidst dominant cultures from Ohiyesa's book *The Soul of the Indian.*

Solitary Communion with Nature

On page 6, Ohiyesa writes about solitary communion with the unseen, which he calls the "highest expression of our religious life." He describes it with the word *bambeday*, literally "mysterious feeling," which has been variously translated as "fasting" and "dreaming." He writes, "It may be better interpreted as 'consciousness of the divine.'...At the solemn hour of sunrise (the Indian) took up his position overlooking the glories of earth and facing the 'Great Mystery' and there he remained, naked, erect, silent, and motionless, exposed to the elements and forces of His arming for a night and a day to two days and nights" (6).

From the chapter on trance-based learning, we know the power of hypnotic receptivity in meditation and intentional awareness. Here, with Ohiyesa's reference to the traditional vision quest in Nature, we are reminded that we can interact with Nature even if all we can access is the night sky. If smog or light pollution makes seeing the night sky impossible, we can look for the sun's penetrating rays or give attention to the falling rain or a procession of ants in the garage. The "dreaming" or trance focus in concert with feeling one with the other-than-human energy enhances the inner benefits of the meditative state even if only an indoor plant is significantly honored as part of the endeavor.

This focus on trance utilization and metacognition reminds us that our separation from Nature is not just a physical one. More importantly, it is a mental one.

> We are mentally, more than physically, isolated from the natural world. The disconnected way we think is polluted and produces behavior that pollutes natural and social systems. We seldom recognize the need for our thinking to be genuinely connected with nature, be renewed, and contribute to life's welfare as part of nature's restorative processes. (Cohen 45)

The shamans of the Achuar and other tribes in Amazonia make solitude a primary part of their healing rituals. Many tribal cultures use vision quests that are solitary events. Until we are alone with ourselves and the natural world, we do not realize the clutter, noise, business and artificial diversions that surround us and addict us to becoming more and more alienated from our roots.

Loving as an Extension of our Relationship With Nature

Referring to Dakota rituals about Father Sun and Mother Earth as "wholly symbolic," Ohiyesa writes: "Therefore our reverence and love for (plants and men) was really an imaginative extension of our love for our immediate parents and with this sentiment of filial piety was joined a willingness to appeal to them as to a father for such good gifts as we may desire" (11). This can be a difficult concept to grasp with dominant worldview thinking and English words, as we learned in the previous chapter. The idea is that from the generosity and gifts of life given by the sun and the earth, we experience love at its essence. From this unending generosity, we ourselves learn how to love one another and to be generous. D. H. Lawrence, perhaps the first prominent Western writer to challenge the dominant worldview and its anthropocentrism, wrote the following poem a year before his death in 1929, which expresses this idea and explains that at the core of human love is our connection to Nature:

> Oh, what a catastrophe, what a maiming of love when it was made personal, merely personal feeling. This is what is the matter with us: we are bleeding at the roots because we are cut off from the earth and sun and stars. Love has become a grinning mockery because, poor blossom, we plucked it from its stem on the Tree of Life and expected it to keep on blooming in our civilized vase on the table. (110)[6]

Ohiyesa also tells how solitude in Nature was a part of marriage and birthing for his people. Speaking of a mother giving birth in the wilderness, he writes: "Tis love! 'tis love! The fulfilling of life! When a sacred voice comes to her out of the silence and a pair of eyes open upon her in the wilderness, she knows with joy that she has born well her great song of creation" (25). As for consummation of the marriage between father and mother, he writes: "We believed that two who love should be united in secret, before the public acknowledgment of their union, and should taste their apotheosis alone with nature" (30). How much better might we treat the world and one another if we had started our lives and our sacred unions amidst the splendor of the natural world! Since we have not, however, we can use our Medicine Wheel to help us reconnect to Nature by being ever mindful of opportunities to reframe or counterbalance the negative thinking or behaviors we bump into or demonstrate with a conscious realization of this loving relationship that is always close by. Even in the most bleak inner city environment, Nature can be located. A moment in the sun or rain or snow with an informed understanding of the living essence and gifts of these spiritual "People" (the sun, rain, snow, plants, etc.) can bring us to a higher consciousness in magical ways when we use both cognitive and imaginative ideation in metaphysical participation with Nature.

Respect for the First Teachers

Closely related to respect for the physical and metaphysical love that Nature represents is an authentic belief in the wisdom imparted by other-than-human relatives who were on the earth prior to us. Ohiyesa writes:

> The Indian loved to come into sympathy and spiritual communion with his brothers of the animal kingdom, whose inarticulate souls had for him something of the sinless purity that we attribute to the innocent and irresponsible child. He had faith in their instincts as in a mysterious wisdom given from above.... Ever seeking to establish spiritual comradeship with the animal creation, the Indian adopted this or that animal as his "totem." The symbolic attribute of beaver, bear, or tortoise, such as wisdom, cunning, courage and the like, was supposed to be mysteriously conferred upon the wearer of the badge. (13, 47)

Consider the nature of a relationship you or someone you know has with a pet. Whether a dog, cat, horse, hamster, pig or parrot, it usually reveals a mutual and unconditional love, with both generosity and loyalty being demonstrated daily. Add to this the knowledge most pet owners have about the unique forms of intelligence, intuition, and virtue their animals possess. Think about what people have learned or could learn about life from their pets. Now imagine having such sentiment and awareness regarding all of Nature's life forms. We may not find loyalty per se in an observed cockroach or in a pigeon passing by without some deep metaphysical awareness and biological knowledge. However, if and when you begin to sincerely consider thinking of other-than-human life as teachers, you will be surprised. Even without the daily contact, responsibility, and intimacy of a pet relationship, the perspective of relatedness can still begin to resurface if your only wildlife is a mouse who is keeping you up at night. In the words of Dene elder George Blondin, "We are people of the land; we see ourselves as no different than the trees, the caribou, and the raven, except we are more complicated" (18). We are no longer people of the land, but we can employ the same logic with whatever Nature we can find. In his book *Living in Two Worlds,* Ohiyesa expands on the important lessons children learn from Nature, describing an Indian mother who:

> . . . humbly seeks to learn a lesson from ants, bees, spiders, beavers, and badgers. She studies the family life of the birds, so exquisite in its emotional intensity and its patient devotion, until she seems to feel the universal mother-heart beating in her own breast. In due time the child takes of his own accord the attitude of prayer, and speaks reverently of the Powers. He thinks that he is a blood brother to all living creatures, and the storm wind is to him a messenger of the "Great Mystery." (43)

When I paddle board around the island in front of my house, I often see some collection of brown and white pelicans, frigates, blue-footed boobies, cormorants, ibis, vultures, and sandpipers sitting together on boulders or trees. It always reminds of how easy it should be for us to get along with others who look different in some way. The birds have no intention of teaching us directly, so we must do the greater part to learn from their behaviors. According to Joseph Epes Brown in his book *Animals of the Soul,* the Oglala "purposefully studied the habits and qualities of the animals in their habitat, and they used the lessons they learned to become skillful hunters who thrived on the plains" (Brown xi). He goes on to say that such study of environmental relationships was about far more than mere physical sustenance: "The Oglala's observations of animal traits were a prime medium through which core values of their culture could find expression . . . the values of generosity, creativity and strength seem not to be projected onto the bison but to emanate from it" (Brown xii). The list of what we can learn from watching animals is endless. In addition to books like Brown's text, there are multiple sites on the Internet with different lists, so it is good that people are thinking about this phenomenon. For example, onegreenplanet .org has an online piece titled "10 Important Life Lessons We Can Learn from Animals" that refers to how we can learn about:

- Compassion in the form of interspecies friendships or foster parenting
- Natural rhythms that cultivate patience
- Living in the present
- Interconnectedness and interdependence
- Recognizing similarities to encourage respect for diversity
- Respect for elders
- Living lightly on the planet or within one's means
- Importance of solidarity

Care2.com also has "Ten Lessons We Can Learn from Animals," which offers some others:

- Ability to forgive and forget
- Not worrying about what others think
- Loving unconditionally
- Trusting instincts
- Playing fair
- Relaxing
- Expressing your uniqueness
- Sharing
- Not giving up

Sometimes animals show up at the right time to teach us important lessons. If we are aware of any unusual creature and can learn about its unique attributes, we can find solutions to many challenges. Such showing-up is especially likely when trance-based learning, such as that associated with a vision quest, is engaged. I offer a personal story as an example:

I was living in Fairfield, Idaho, adjacent to the Saw Tooth National Mountains. It was early July and I was preparing to do a Wiwanki Wacipi (Sun Dance) to be held on the Pine Ridge Reservation in South Dakota. I had just heard that the temperatures during the time of the four-day ceremony were predicted to get as high as 112 degrees. I had completed two or three other Sun Dances but a subtle fear overtook me nonetheless. No longer living on the reservation, I perhaps felt I was not sufficiently acclimated to the heat. In any case, as the days went on, my concern, my "fear," grew. Perhaps, I thought, I would have an experience that would help me get rid of it when I went up into the mountains for my hanbleceya ("crying for a vision"), also known as a vision quest.

I found my special place atop a flat spot on a rocky pinnacle overlooking the prairie far below. I set down my circle of tobacco ties and stepped inside with my pipe. After I had been sitting quietly for a few minutes, a rat-like rodent stepped out of the woods and started nibbling on one of the ties to get to the tobacco. Instinctively, I kicked my foot out to chase it away. As it scurried back into the woods I realized my mistake. I had fallen into my Post PoD mindset, forgetting that the greatest teachings of an hanbleceya came from animals.

Feeling I had blown it and would spend the rest of my hours regretting my error, I watched my fears about the Sun Dance grow. I did my best to regroup by praying. Suddenly, the creature returned. This time, however, he stepped into the circle with me and turned to face the west as I was. He acted as if he were my pet or my watchdog. Now I knew this was my "vision." After a short while, he scooted back to the tobacco, had a few bites, and moved back into the woods with one jump. I noted his unusually large legs and long tail. For the rest of the time, I rejoiced and dreamed about my new friend. I knew throughout the night that it had brought me exactly what I needed to learn to overcome my fear. Still, owing to my ignorance and loss of the Indigenous knowledge of place I should have had, I could barely wait to get to my computer!

When I eventually returned to my house, I started the fire for the inipi and then ran upstairs to my computer. My wife was surprised but could not talk to me until I got out of the purification lodge. I Googled "Rodents of North America" and "Idaho varieties of rats" under images, and there he was. A "Kangaroo Rat." Then I searched to learn more about it. I did not have a local shaman to teach me. Using the computer was my only choice, as I did not have the knowledge about the creatures where I lived that Indigenous wisdom requires. Then the lesson hit me when I came upon one site that read something like, "They don't need to drink." It said the animal was of the genus Dipodomys and could go a lifetime without drinking a drop of water. I laughed, prayed for the world and gave my gratitude in the lodge, and emerged ready for the heat and lack of water I would soon face.

■■■■

Respect for the Relatives Who Nurture Us

Ohiyesa writes that respect for the life and spirit of the other-than-human nations includes how one views the taking of plants, animals, birds, and fish for food. Speaking of the American Indian in the third person, he writes: "His respect for the immortal part of the animal, his brother, often leads him so far as to lay out the body of his game in state and decorate the head with symbolic paint or feathers" (47). Under the Indigenous worldview, humans do not have "dominion" over plants and animals. Instead, it reveals that:

- ■ We live in a cooperative community with them as well as with the spirits in the rocks, rivers and stars.

- We are related in direct and indirect ways that recognize interdependence.
- We cannot live without them.
- We are equals among them and that each has its own soul or spiritual essence, as we do.
- We are indebted to them as our teachers because they were here first.
- We must make generosity and respect the most important part of the relationship on behalf of the greater good of all.

Of course, a number of people in dominant cultures have views about "animal rights." However, sometimes even with sincere proponents of this idea, anthropocentric assumptions fall short of the Indigenous sense of equality of species. Human dominance and dominion are still paramount, and therefore economic choices can continue the destruction of habitats. The loss of our Indigenous worldview paradigm, in spite of the animal rights movement, has allowed for how terribly we treat our living food sources in general. Too many still buy chicken raised in small boxes or feedlot cows. Respect and empathy for the fish we catch is often lacking, and few feel a profound interpersonal appreciation for the corn we eat, a plant that represents cosmic powers to many First Nations. We must more carefully consider the worldview we hold that motivates our belief in animal or plant "rights" because the dominant worldview's influence creates significant inconsistencies we otherwise miss. This allows for a more prevailing mindset such as that promoted by economist Murray N. Rothbard. Read this paragraph from his 2007 piece "The 'Rights' of Animals" and reflect on how your own economic, philosophical, or spiritual orientation connects to it even if there are exceptions in your mind:

> Individuals possess rights *not* because we "feel" that they should, but because of a rational inquiry into the nature of man and the universe. In short, man has rights because they are *natural* rights. They are grounded in the nature of man: the individual man's capacity for conscious choice, the necessity for him to use his mind and energy to adopt goals and values, to find out about the world, to pursue his ends in order to survive and prosper, his capacity and need to communicate and interact with other human beings and to participate in the division of labor. In short, man is a rational and social animal. No other animals or beings possess this ability to reason, to make conscious choices, to transform their environment in order to prosper, or to collaborate consciously in society and the division of labor. From this perspective everything about our relationship to other life forms on Earth are relative *to the species man*. A rights-ethic for mankind is precisely and only for humans. The Biblical story was insightful to the effect that man was "given"—or, in

natural law, we may say "has"—dominion over all the species of the earth. Natural law is necessarily species-bound. (n.p.)

Rothbard, although known as a free-market libertarian, nonetheless finds support for his words in the general capitalistic system. As long as externalities like costs of production passed on to others without their consent, such as water and air pollution, are part of the economic system, Rothbard's ideas will be supported. An Indigenous worldview that considers "resources" as "relatives" has no place in modern capitalism. And rationalizations about only humans having choice-making ability are supported by Aristotle's ideas about reason (*logos*) existing only in man. Even though he believed that man had perception, Descarte's mechanistic philosophy reduced that to reflex. Darwin, whose ideas about the primitiveness of Indigenous Peoples we visited previously, at least challenged Descarte on this, offering in *Origin of Species* that "It is a significant fact, that the more the habits of any particular animal are studied by a naturalist, the more he attributes to reason, and the less to unlearnt instinct" (46).

There may be increasing interest among philosophers and some scientists in studying whether or not other-than-human life has consciousness, but they will always fall short of the empirical evidence cultivated from the observation across millions of years that informs the Indigenous worldview. With its guidance, we do not have to wait while we continue each day allowing hundreds of species to go extinct. We can continue abiding by the Thanksgiving prayer offered in the Preface to start this book's journey. We can continue it for all of life with awareness of the other-than-human consciousness that is behind what even the fish are doing in the world:

> We turn out thoughts to all of the Fish life in the water. They were instructed to cleanse and purify the water. They also give themselves to us as food. We are grateful that they continue to their duties and we send to the Fish our greetings and our thanks. Now our minds are one. (Kimmerer 109)

Moral Education and Nature

In another section of *The Soul of an Indian* entitled "And the Moral Code," Ohiyesa writes:

> As a child I understood how to give; I have forgotten that grace since I became civilized. I lived the natural life, whereas I now live the artificial.... Any pretty pebble was valuable to me then; every growing tree an object of reverence. Now I worship with the white man before painted landscapes whose value is estimated in dollars. (86)

Then in a section entitled "The Unwritten Scriptures," he explains: "Naturally magnanimous and open-minded, the red man prefers to believe that the Spirit of God is not breathed into man alone, but that the whole created universe is a sharer in the immortal perfection of its Maker" (89). Such observations imply that morality stems not from humans but from the Nature of which we are part. This view of morality does not find its way into most approaches to teaching virtues under the dominant worldview. Peter Smagorinsky and Joel Taxel recognize this in their study of character education programs in the United States. Referring to a book on an Indigenous approach to character education that my daughter Jessica and I wrote, they state: "Our views prior to conducting this study have not remained entirely intact" (346). They go on to identify how our Indigenous approach was significantly different from all the others they studied:

> In *Teaching Virtues: Building Character across the Curriculum* Native American educators Don Trent Jacobs and Jessica Jacobs-Spencer (2001) outline a perspective on character education that is different in fundamental ways from either approach we have described. In particular, they view character as extending beyond human communities and encompassing "intimate relationships of living things" (p. vii). This belief in the interrelations among all constituents of the ecology extends to those earthly objects viewed in the West as inanimate... A major goal... is for students "to internalize virtues as part of their identity and learn how this identity relates to the larger web of life" (p. vii). The distinguishing premises of this perspective are as follows:
>
> - All Life and Nature Are Interconnected. Here Jacobs and Jacobs-Spencer offer a possibility not available through Western conceptions of character, the idea that moral relationships extend to the natural environment...
> - Character Education Includes the Spiritual Realm. In American Indian cultures, this sacred aspect of the child is nurtured from birth so that the sense of interconnections colors all of the person's subsequent learning...
> - Character Education is Built on Universal Virtues. Such facets of character as feeling humility, being at peace, being spiritual, seeing generosity as the highest expression of courage, and feeling connected with all life forms are absent from Western conceptions of character... invoking different traditions and resulting in different conceptions of a good society. (60)

An Alternative to Churches

Ohiyesa, who became a Christian, refers often to "God" as the Great Mysterious(ing) and scoffs at the idea that whatever creative energy is responsible for Nature would not require a man-made structure as his "house" or a place for us to visit with his/her spiritual energies. In spite of Ohiyesa's Christian indoctrination, he is clear that for him Nature, not churches, make for the more logical meeting place: "He would deem it

sacrilege to build a house for Him who may be met face to face in the mysterious, shadowy aisles of the primeval forest, or on the sunlit bosom of virgin
prairies, upon dizzy spires and pinnacles of naked rock, and yonder in the
jeweled vault of the night sky!" (Ohiyesa 3). He goes on to say, "I believe
Christianity and modern civilization are opposed and irreconcilable, and
that the spirit of Christianity and of our ancient religion is essentially the
same" (Ohiyesa 4). Not all Indigenous scholars agree with his belief that Indigenous spirituality and Christianity have a similar essence. For example,
Robert Allen Warrior, a member of the Osage Nation, writes that "the *Bible*
will always be incompatible with authentic Indigenous ways of seeing the
world" (Warrior 263). Yet Ohiyesa was also critical of the religion itself:

> Yet the religion that is preached in our churches and practiced by our con-
> gregations, with its element of display and self-aggrandizement, its active
> proselytism, and its open contempt of all religions but its own, was for a long
> time extremely repellent. To his simple mind, the professionalism of the
> pulpit, the paid exhorter, the moneyed church, was unspiritual and unedify-
> ing and it was not until his spirit was broken and his moral and physical con-
> stitution undermined by trade, conquest, and strong drink, that Christian
> missionaries obtained any real hold upon him. (Ohiyesa 6)

In my peer-reviewed article *False Doctrine and the Stifling of Indigenous
Political Will*, I make the point that "there is a correlation between the fail-
ure of Indigenous politics to achieve its goals and the sway of what Thomas
Paine refers to as the false doctrine of Christian dogma" (Four Arrows 1).
Churches are fine for social events and dialogue among humans, but until
they are endowed with ample other-than-human life systems with which to
commune, they will continue only to separate us from Nature as a source of
everything we need socially, mentally, psychologically, physically and spiritually. Why not arrange for people to meet outdoors where plants, birds,
insects, and clouds can be part of the experience? If such accommodation
is impossible, perhaps a park or some other place where some authentic
engagement with the other-than-human world can work. Meeting in a purification lodge (house of vapor) can work well, as it incorporates the sacred
use of fire, water, air, and rock, while evoking natural spirits and facilitating
physical transformations via the heat and darkness. Even if some churches
have abundant indoor plants, the sermons and Sunday school sessions can
do far more to bring Nature into the focus on sacred things. This is not to
say that people of various faiths cannot enter into dialogue with the spirit
world in a man-made structure. I agree with Ohiyesa that the founders of
most of the dominant religions understood the invisible world in ways that
are at least complementary, if not similar, to Indigenous spirituality. However, until we can re-embrace Nature as part of the "More than Human

World" that David Abram refers to in the subtitle of his book *Spell of the Sensual*, religions will likely continue to support the current war on Nature in one way or another.[7]

It may also be useful to note that Indigenous ceremonies and rituals that relate to success in hunting, personal healing, or other desires on the physical plane are understood as belonging to a somewhat lower order than strictly spiritual ones, where becoming one with all and living in the highest way for the good of all are the focus. Ohiyesa makes this point in *Soul of the Indian*:

> The red man divided mind into two parts—the spiritual mind and the physical mind. The first is pure spirit, concerned only with the essence of things, and it was this he sought to strengthen by spiritual prayer, during which the body is subdued by fasting and hardship. In this type of prayer there was no beseeching favor or help. All matters of personal or selfish concern, as success in hunting or warfare, relief from sickness, or the sparing of a beloved life, were definitely relegated to the plane of the lower or material mind, and all ceremonies, charms, or incantations designed to secure a benefit or to avert a danger, were recognized as emanating from the physical self. (8)

I will never forget watching a PBS television special of a presentation Joseph Campbell made where he described an Indigenous creation story. (I cannot remember what tribe and have searched in vain to find a reference to this presentation). At the end of his presentation he got so choked up he almost cried as he uttered, "Compare that to Genesis!" *In The Truth about Stories*, Thomas King similarly compares Genesis and an Aboriginal creation story:

> A theologian might argue that these two creation stories are essentially the same. Each tells about the creation of the world and the appearance of human beings. But a storyteller would tell you that these two stories are quite different.... Elements in Genesis create a particular universe governed by a series of hierarchies... that celebrate law, order, and good government, while in our Native story, the universe is governed by a series of co-operations... that celebrate equality and balance. (23–24)

Finding Complementarity (When Possible)

Ohiyesa's ability to live in two worlds and his notions about Christianity and Indigenous spirituality being potentially complementary illustrate one of the most important reasons a "Nature as All" worldview component is part of this book's five Medicine Wheel teachings. Ohiyesa reminds us to consciously look at the similarities and differences among most things as being symbiotic in some way. Cultures, beliefs, religions, ideologies, food choices, languages, and so forth provide a diversity whose complementarity can make everything stronger. Just like Chinese Rice and Kansas wheat can together sustain more challenging weather than either can do alone, such different things can make us all stronger.

In fact, I believe that discrimination against Nature because of a general belief in human superiority sets the foundation for human discrimination against other humans. Just as Nature and all that is in it is imbued with spirit, soul and a selfhood, so too are those whom we call enemies. If we can engage in authentic complementary relationships with rocks, rivers, roses, and rabbits, we can begin to get along with one another in spite of differences. This is why I invited Walter Block, a Loyola professor who fully agrees with Rothbard that only humans have intrinsic value, to write a book with me. While writing *Differing Worldviews in Higher Education*, we became friends and found common ground.[8] Imagine the trees and bees as Peoples of a different order, as you might a Martian who lands a spaceship in front of you.

One reason searching for complementarity is difficult is because of the mythologies that inform the two different worldviews. I have written elsewhere about how all cultures under both worldviews have twin-hero mythology.[9] Usually, one twin is direct, strong, and aggressive, representing solar energy, whereas the other is indirect, reflective, and passive, representing lunar energy. In the dominant culture's stories, the solar twin kills or overshadows the lunar twin, as in the stories of Romulus and Remus, Cain and Able, Jacob and Esau, and Hercules and Iphicles. But in Indigenous stories, the twins work in solidarity and harmony. When the Navajo solar twin named Monster Slayer wants to shoot an arrow into the Monster with the Long Arms, his lunar twin named Child Born of the Water suggests they sing to him instead. They do and the monster, never having been treated this way, lets them pass. Just as animals teach complementarity in many stories, it is not a coincidence that animals are crucial parts of this and other Indigenous origin myths.[10] We must create new myths and stories to revitalize our unconscious psyche and work hard at finding complementarity.

The idea that finding balance in apparent opposites is an important law is emphasized in Mary Graham's study of Australian Aborigines. In her paper "Thoughts about the Philosophical Underpinnings of Aboriginal Worldviews," this Aboriginal scholar and Kombu-Merri person explains that cultural manifestations about living on this planet are and will always be multiple and subject to an eventual balancing of opposites. As she explains, this is the only way to live in harmony with creatures so different from us:

> Aboriginal Law is grounded in the perception of a psychic level of natural behaviour, the behaviour of natural entities. Aboriginal people maintain

that humans are not alone. They are connected and made by way of relationships with a wide range of beings, and it is thus of prime importance to maintain and strengthen these relationships. . . . The land, and how we treat it, is what determines our human-ness. Because land is sacred and must be looked after, the relation between people and land becomes the template for society and social relations. (107)

Writing a book in which I emphasize strong contrasts and preferences between two worldviews may seem to be a contradiction with the Indigenous principle of complementarity. Yet seeking complementarity in all apparent opposites also calls for realizing that not all opposites allow for such symbiosis. The Quechua-speaking peoples of the Andean Mountains in Peru agree. In describing a research project in her publication "The Splendid and the Savage: The Dance of the Opposites in Indigenous Andean Thought," Hillary S. Webb offers a comprehensive analysis of the meaning of three of their words: *yanantin, masintin,* and *chuya* (69–93). "Yanantin" describes the idea of a universal oneness that includes an understanding of a sort of pairing of opposites. "Masintin" is "the active process by which the yanantin pair becomes 'paired' and thus moves from a state of antagonism and separateness to one of complementarity and interdependence" (74). The word "chuya" refers to an entity that may be missing its potential complementary other or that is still viewed as being unequal somehow. Even with regards to the oneness of yanantin, however, she learned that the Natives say that not all apparent opposites are suitable for pairing. Harrison, another researcher of yanantin, concurs:[11] "Quechua speakers persistently distinguish objects which are not well matched or 'equal'" (149).

This situation does not mean that the prophesied reunion of the white and red brother is not possible or that we cannot find complementarity in the great variety of cultures, religions, ideologies, and practices. It means that at the level of worldview, there may be only one way to describe the water in which we swim in terms of its most essential components and that, for now at least, the one that has proven long-term success in maintaining harmonious life systems is the one we had before our point of departure.

Conclusion

The Indigenous worldview is literally rooted in the earth. It is about interconnected relationships across the spectrum of the visible and invisible universe. The dominant worldview is attached to economics, objectification, and rationalism. It is about categorizing and hierarchy. For 99 percent of human history, at least in the current world we inhabit,[12] we managed to live in accord with the laws of Nature, and life systems on the planet were healthy. Today our references to other-than-humans are mostly utilitarian-oriented. These beings are "natural resources" obtained for our pleasure, their uses ranging from food to pets. Animals are dissected to find new pharmaceutical drugs or to better understand human systems for the advancement of medicine, and the spirit in plants has been all but ignored. Today researchers trying to solve our ecological crises look at the movement of animals and insects to find shortcuts to getting things done quickly regardless of the outcomes. In an article published in the journal *Digital Information Management* entitled "Wolf Search Algorithm with Ephemeral Memory," Fong and colleagues write in their abstract, "Researchers recently have invented a collection of heuristic optimization methods inspired by the movements of animals and insects (e.g., Firefly, Cuckoos, Bats) with the advantages of efficient computation and easy implementation" (167). A description of "heuristic" on Wikipedia says: "The objective of a heuristic is to produce a solution in a reasonable time frame that is good enough for solving the problem at hand. This solution may not be the best of all the actual solutions to this problem, or it may simply approximate the exact solution." Does this sound like a solid way to address mass extinction?

This does not mean that Indigenous wisdom cannot be used in corporate settings if it honors the more holistic perspective of the worldview. I once had a doctoral student who came to me with the hope of finding something in some Indigenous approaches to learning that might assist him as a specialist in "expert knowledge transfer" at Intel. We came up with a way for outgoing senior PhDs to storify their knowledge according to animal-based Indigenous story structures and symbolism. This included widening the circle of people who would be interactively involved in the storytelling, such as secretaries, janitors, and so on. In his abstract, he writes:

> I attempted to see if an approach to this process that is more holistic than is typical in business and industry might be more successful. Specifically, I applied traditional indigenous methods for transferring knowledge from those who have mastery in a given field. The purpose of this study was to use indigenous approaches to oral storytelling as a teaching technique for solving specific problems in technical learning for semiconductor engineers and then to compare and contrast outcomes.... The root-cause analysis resulted in 12 explanations, four assessment items (morals), and a final score of 4.0 (based on a 5.0 scale), with an increase perceived mean score of 43.75% in technical capability. Indigenous storytelling appears to have significant advantages over standard industry protocols that seem to allow experts and learners to see how things really are without reality being overly filtered through individual ego. (Spaulding 9)

I grant that the Indigenous worldview that perceives all of Nature as sacred comes from observations and practices unique to localities that took thousands of years to develop into cultural wisdom, and I concede that carefully orchestrated ceremony and communication with the spirit world along with extensive life skill practice are needed to fully embrace and live according to such wisdom. However, the DNA of this wisdom is in us all, and we can relearn relatively quickly at least enough to possibly protect the seventh generation for what otherwise lies ahead. If it is too late, perhaps we can do enough to help its members with the rebuilding. The places of power still hold spiritual energy and are waiting for us to respect them again. We can begin with more concentrated efforts to watch the sun rise and set, giving thanks for each day, or to contemplate the star and moon cycles or the oceans tides. We can study the weeds growing through the sidewalk with a new reverence or can tune into the vibrations of a local tree and the life that interacts with it. Learning about places in which we live and their histories can also help reconnect us to them. Rethinking about the life of insects before stomping on them can open our hearts to a more empathetic solution. Choosing food more consciously and knowing from where it came can also be life changing in many ways.

The list of how we can reconnect with a "Nature as All" orientation goes on. The point is we must renew our focus on Nature in every possible way now. We must pay more attention to the land, plants and animals, waters, skies, cosmos, and invisible spiritual energies that exist everywhere. Even if you are sitting in front of a TV screen watching a movie, pause to reflect on how it does or does not honor Nature. Notice how denial of reality and separation from it happens continually via our media and schools. In her book *Communicating Nature: How We Create and Understand Environmental Messages,* Julia B. Corbe writes that it is our everyday communications that form our perceptions of the natural world and lead to a better understanding of the cultural context of human–nature interactions. Such attention to how we communicate is augmented by a worldview that understands that a spiritual energy constantly in motion connects everything we do.[13] If we look at skill acquisition and/or personal transformation not as ways to gain more money, power, or prestige, but as ways to bring spiritual awareness to our environment, perhaps we can begin to take care of it again. Walk into the most natural environment you can locate and seek such awareness by focusing on whatever draws your attention, and then look, listen, and feel for some important meaning that you can apply to your life. Use trance-based learning and be open to the synchronicity of animal and plant symbolism that you either intuit or can learn from others, while always remembering that your highest authority is honest reflection itself. Make sure your communication with self and others minimizes categorical thinking and hierarchy and emphasizes movement and potential. Be courageous in using what you learn from Nature in word and deed to bring balance back into the world with the future generations in mind.

"The CAT and FAWN Connection"

As some readers may know and as I have mentioned in an explanatory note or two, this book's five chapter topics and how they are connected in our Medicine Wheel first came to me in 1997 as a vision shortly after I experienced a near-death event while kayaking the Rio Urique in Mexico's Copper Canyon. After surviving being sucked into an underground hole through which the entire river drained, two animals that I encountered during our climb out of the canyon were a rare wolf-like cat known as an onza and a young fawn. The onza was alive and walked over my sleeping bag where I lay in a cave above the rising waters. The fawn was carried by a Raramuri Indian who had run it down and clubbed it to feed his family.[14] The vision turned the two animals into the words "CAT" and "FAWN." Years of reflection on what turned out to be a life-changing transformation brought me to conclude that CAT symbolized "Concentration-Activated Transformation," which I understood as "trance-based learning." FAWN represented how the dominant worldview understandings of Fear, Authority, Words, and Nature were destroying our world because of how the understandings interacted with CAT. Moreover, the Indigenous understandings about FAWN were nearly opposite and offered ways we could reverse the destruction and regain our balance. The chapters of this book have reintroduced CAT-FAWN but with new insights into the two worldviews that can guide a more widespread metacognitive effort on behalf of changing our dominant worldview beliefs about the interactions between the five components presented in this book. If the reader uses this unique Medicine Wheel and its interactions to consider daily choices, feelings, problems and deep-seated beliefs, my vision tells me we have a chance to help restore the world for the seventh generation. Now it is up to you.

Notes

1. My contributing authors and I address this in *Unlearning the Language of Conquest* in a footnote to the quotation (xiii).
2. See *Indian Notebooks (1847–1861) of Henry D. Thoreau,* transcribed with an Introduction and additional material by Richard F. Fleck (2007).
3. I contend that in addition to this support of one of our Medicine Wheel philosophies about language, this work of his also developed his sense of courage.

Recall the famous story about how, when Thoreau practiced civil disobedience and was put in jail, his friend Ralph Waldo Emerson asked, "What are you doing in there?" and the reply was "Waldo, what are you doing out there?"

4. The conflict resulted in the largest mass execution in American history when the state of Minnesota hanged thirty-eight Dakota (Linder). (Only the unpopular intervention of Lincoln saved another 235 condemned prisoners.) The next year, the state forcibly removed all Lakota and Dakota. The boy's father was released from prison by Lincoln around this time.

5. Vine was also knowledgeable about "anti-Indianism," having contributed to my edited text *Unlearning the Language of Conquest* one of the last chapters he wrote before he passed on. It is titled "Conquest Masquerading as Law."

6. Just as Thoreau's writings (as we see later) stemmed from his intentional exploration and support of the Indigenous worldview, it appears that D.H. Lawrence's writing was also strongly influenced by his Indigenous worldview studies, first with the Australian Aborigines and then with the American Indians of New Mexico starting around 1922 (Game).

7. It may be useful to note here that Indigenous People understand that religious/spiritual ceremonies are events of a relatively lower order when they relate to the physical world.

8. We still have major disagreements, but I think we are both better people for having done the work, and our audiences have learned much about cooperative argumentation. To listen to our presentation at St. Louis University, search for Four Arrows and Walter Block on YouTube.

9. See *Primal Awareness* (Jacobs). See also the pioneering work of Howard Teich in this arena.

10. See how water beetles, spiders, ravens, eagles, plant seeds and so forth played instrumental roles in most twin-hero and origin myths in Barbara C. Sproul's *Primal Myths: Creation Myths around the World* (1979) and in Michael Hutchins's edited *Grzimek's Animal Life Encyclopedia: Evolution*. Web.

11. There are many parts of Western cultures, beliefs and philosophies that can find complementarity in many Indigenous counterparts. A worldview that sees no value in other-than-humans except as a resource may have created things of complementary value even though in itself it may not be complementary to the original understandings.

12. A number of Indigenous cultures believe as do the Hopi that we are entering into a "fifth world." They believe that human separation from the laws of Nature led to the destruction of the first three worlds and that we may be close to doing the same for the present fourth world. So when I say humans have lived in relative harmony for 99 percent of our history, I refer to the time we have been living in this fourth world up until around 9,000 years ago at our point of departure.

13. See also Kari Norgaard's *Living in Denial: Climate Change, Emotions and Everyday Life* (2011) and Robert Cox's *Environmental Communication and the Public Sphere* (2010).

14. The story itself originally appears in my book *Primal Awareness: A True Story of Survival, Awakening, and Transformation with the Raramuri Shamans of Mexico* (1998). It also introduces differences between dominant and Indigenous be-

liefs about fear, authority, words and Nature but without the depth and new associations brought forth in this book. There is also a video I hope to upload to YouTube of my two visits to Copper Canyon, one when the near-death event and the vision occurred and the other whereby I learned "The Shaman's Message," the name of the video narrating more than a hundred photos and accompanied by original Tarahumara music.

Recommended Reading About Indigenous Worldview

Abram, D. (1997). *The spell of the sensuous: Perception and language in a more-than-human world.* New York, NY: Vintage.

Atleo, R. (2005). *Tsawalk: A Nuu-chah-nulth worldview.* Vancouver, BC: University of British Columbia Press.

Bastien, B., & Mistaken Chief, D. (2004). *Blackfoot ways of knowing: The worldview of the Siksikaitsitapi.* Calgary, AB: University of Calgary Press.

Cajete, G. (1994). *Look to the mountain. An ecology of Indigenous education.* Skyland, NC: Kivaki Press.

Corbett, J. B. (2006). *Communicating nature: How we create and understand environmental messages.* Washington, DC: Island Press.

Deloria, Jr., V. (1999). *Spirit and reason.* New York, NY: Fulcrum.

Four Arrows, D., Cajete, G., & Lee, J. (2010). *Critical neurophilosophy and Indigenous wisdom.* New York, NY: Sense Publishing

Four Arrows, D. (2013). *Teaching truly: A curriculum to Indigenize mainstream education.* New York, NY: Peter Lang

Four Arrows, D. (2010). *Unlearning the language of conquest: Scholars expose anti-Indianism in America.* Austin, TX: University of Texas Press.

Gill, J. H. (2002). *Native American worldviews: An introduction.* New York, NY: Humanity Press.

Gross, L. W. (2014). *Anishinaabe ways of knowing and being.* Farnham, UK: Ashgate Publishing.

Herman, Louis G. (2013). *Future primal: How our wilderness origins show us the way forward.* Novato, CA: New World Library.

Point of Departure, pages 141–142

Jacobs, Don. T. (1998). *Primal Awareness: A True Story of Survival, Awakening and Transformation with the Raramuri Shamans of Mexico.* Rochester, VT: Inner Traditions.

Kawagley, A. O. (2006). *A Yupiaq worldview: A pathway to ecology and spirit.* Long Grove, IL: Waveland Press.

Kelsey, P. M. (2010). *Tribal theory in Native American literature: Dakota and Haudenosaunee writing and Indigenous worldviews.* Lincoln, NE: University of Nebraska Press.

Kimmerer, R. W. (2015). *Braiding Sweetgrass: Indigenous wisdom, scientific knowledge and the teachings of plants.* Minneapolis, MN: Milkweed Publishers

Kramer, E., Adkins, G., Kim, S. H., & Miller, G. (2014). *Environmental communication and the extinction vortex: Technology as denial of death.* Cresskill, NJ: Hampton Press.

Lawlor, R. (1991). *Voices of the first day.* Rochester, VT: Inner Traditions.

Maybury-Lewis, D. M. (1992). *Tribal wisdom and the modern world.* New York, NY: Viking.

McGaa, E. (1990). *Mother Earth spirituality: Native American paths to healing ourselves and our world.* New York, NY: Harper.

Nelso, M. K. (2008). *Original instructions: Indigenous teachings for a sustainable future.* Rochester, VT: Bear and Company.

Peat, F. D. (1994). *Blackfoot physics. A journey into the Native American universe.* London, UK: Fourth Estate.

Pierotti, R. (2011). *Indigenous knowledge, ecology and evolutionary biology.* New York, NY: Routledge.

Plotkin, B. (2007). *Nature and the human soul: Cultivating wholeness and community in a fragmented world.* Novato, CA: New World Library.

Sefa Dei, G. J. (Ed.). (2011). *Indigenous philosophies and critical education: A reader.* New York, NY: Peter Lang.

Shepard, P. (1998). *Coming home to the Pleistocene.* Washington, DC: Island Press.

Vaughan, G. (Ed.). (2007). *Women and the gift economy: A radically different worldview is possible.* Toronto, ON: Inanna Publications and Education.

Weatherford, J. (1988). *Indian givers: How the Indians of the Americas transformed the world.* New York, NY: Fawcett Columbine.

Wildcat, D. (2009). *Red alert! Saving the planet with indigenous knowledge.* Golden, CO: Fulcrum.

Epigraph

In our worldview, we are beings who come from the Earth, from the water, and from corn. The Lenca people are ancestral guardians of the rivers, in turn protected by the spirits of young girls, who teach us that giving our lives in various ways for the protection of the rivers is giving our lives for the well-being of humanity and of this planet. Let us wake up! We're out of time. WE must shake our conscience free of the rapacious capitalism, racism and patriarchy that will only assure our own self-destruction. Our Mother Earth—militarized, fenced-in, poisoned, a place where basic rights are systematically violated—demands that we take action.

—**Berta Cáceres**
Recipient of Goldman Environmental Prize
Assassinated for her activism on March 2, 2016
in her home in Honduras.

Two Personal Stories About Using the CAT and FAWN Medicine Wheel

Story One: Healing Myself

In March of 2008 the UCLA oncology center diagnosed me as having non-Hodgkins lymphoma. Inside my abdomen next to my aorta resided a 6.2 centimeter tumor with a smaller one in my arm pit. After second, third and fourth opinions from top cancer specialists who agreed with the diagnosis but varied in their prescriptions for surgery, radiation, and chemo, I opted to do none of them. Instead, I trusted in the Indigenous worldview Medicine Wheel teachings presented in this book. Eight years later, I can say I have never had a down day from the tumors and the one next to my aorta is now only 2 centimeters in diameter and continuing to shrink, as is the one under my arm. I remain grateful for this gradual process. I figure it likely took a long time for them to grow so I am happy to let them die gracefully. Having turned 70, I still do long distance stand-up paddle boarding, play handball, and mountain bike some fairly rugged terrain. I attribute much of my wellness to my work with the Medicine Wheel's cycles presented in

Point of Departure, pages 145–153
Copyright © 2016 by Information Age Publishing

this book, using its CAT-FAWN components of the Indigenous worldview. Here I briefly describe how I personally use CAT-FAWN in my life.

CAT (Trance-Based Learning)

First, I make trance-based learning (or Concentration Activated Transformation) the center of my treatment program as it is the center of the Medicine Wheel. I use trance consciousness to be continually mindful of opportunities for other-than-human information in all of its mysterious forms, from apparent synchronicities to insights resulting from my participation in sports. For reflection on them, I practice meditation and do purification lodges several times a week. I use self-hypnosis to instill lessons learned. Music is a big part of my life. I play piano and flute and the reader who enjoys old time American popular jazz can go to Youtube and watch my performances at the World Championship Old Time Piano Contest.

I use self-hypnosis daily with a focus on my wellness in behalf of being able to maximize my helping others. Whenever life's challenges or my own inadequacies surface, I use trance-based learning to regroup and to center myself again according to the four directions "FAWN" reminds me to consider in light of Indigenous worldview. My goal is never directly about healing from a "cancer" per se, but rather to engage the assistance of the spirit world to help me be of genuine service to others. In other words my pursuit of being at my highest state of consciousness and health until it is time for me to die so I can continue to make some small contribution to others.

Of course, the trance-based learning must engage the four directions with an Indigenous worldview rather than a dominant one in mind as relates to the four influences on TBL:

Fear and the directions of "Courage and Fearlessness;"
Authority and the direction of Community-based Self -Authorship;"
Words and the direction of "Sacred Communication;"
Nature and the direction of "Nature is All."

Fear and the Directions of Courage and Fearlessness

Fear of death is the first thing to overcome when one is diagnosed with "terminal cancer." Using the Indigenous worldview understanding that fear is an opportunity practicing a virtue shifts, I shifted away from the initial apprehension and shifted the energy by using trance-based learning to focus on becoming more generous, more patient, more courageous, more respectful, more humble, more focused on the greater good, etc. Recall that using fear as a catalysis for practicing a virtue is the goal. Once a full, honest, courageous commitment to doing this was in motion, fearlessness washed over me. I trusted in the universe once I was committed to my game plan. This is a healing process we can do for all of life-systems on earth if our trust is accompanied with the hard work. In my case the hard work was simply getting enough exercise; eating wisely; communicating with the spirit world; getting Vitamin D from the Sun, and doing my best in helping the greater good.

Authority and the Direction of Community-Based Self-Authorship

I must admit that having been raised under the dominant worldview I got sucked into the medical establishment protocols when the "experts" diagnosed me. We all fall for the hegemony that surrounds us if we lose touch with our self-authorship to be healthy so that we can do our best in helping others. It requires believing in a worldview that sees honest reflection on lived experience amidst an interconnected world as the highest authority. For this situation, my own lived experience revealed that most of the time I went to a doctor in my life was a waste of time. In fact, I realized that it made me worse as often as it helped. I concluded that about 80% of the time it made no difference; 10% of the time it made things worse; and 10% of the time it helped. After researching facts about chemotherapy and surgery for cancer, I decided that the potential for more harm than good was much higher than the 10%.

Rather than surgery, radiation and chemotherapy, I became more fully committed to enjoyable exercise twice a day to oxygenate my cells so no more than 17 hours never passed by to give the tumors an anaerobic environment in which to thrive. I got my Vitamin D from the Sun and did not scrub it off learning it took 48 hours to penetrate. I ate with ever more attention to the spirit in foods and selected items not exposed to contamination or disrespect as much as possible. I managed my stress with trance-based work. I took authority for all of my choices under the umbrella of a worldview dictated my independence was intended to serve the greater good.

Taking control of my self-authorship required trance-based learning in all of its forms to both recognize that when I giving authority for my beliefs to someone else. I recognized when the authority came from early childhood beliefs or because cultural hegemony. I used trance work also to instill my metacognitive conclusions so that they were automatically reflected in my thinking and behaviors. If stress came to me, I used self-authorship, courage and trance in concert to realize that I am in control of how I respond to it. I employed humor and engagement with Nature while being mindful of the power of my words to my self-authorship strong.

Self-authorship as understood via Indigenous worldview has also allowed me to seek help from others that I know can be beneficial, such as yoga teachers or nutrition specialists or the professor who has an online lymphoma survival group and shares state-of-the art information. Equally it has allowed me to offer the gift of serving others. In my community I have taught self-hypnosis free of charge to a number of people suffering from physical or mental illnesses or addictions.

Words and the Direction of Sacred Communication

It is amazing how our English words can bring forth fear and lead us to depend on hierarchy and external authority when talking about "cancer" with others. Just saying "I have cancer" itself is problematic. With the Indigenous worldview understanding of sacred communication that is about manifesting transformative potentiality I constantly catch myself and rephrase such "languaging." For example, I don't say "I have cancer." I say I was diagnosed with having a form of it called lymphoma and then go on to describe it in ways that neutralize the stigma and give ample room for transformation and healing. "What a gifting it continues to be," I say. Similarly, when doing the self-hypnosis to focus specifically on healing images and the continual shrinking of the tumors, I take care to use positive, verb-based language. I refer to systems becoming more and more healthy and doing what they need to do as I meet them halfway with my lifestyle and thinking. I remember to say that my goal is only to be a better person in all ways and my words about the tumors always involve them doing what they can best do to help me become my highest self and help others.

Nature and the Direction of Nature is All

I realize that my living on the ocean near a remote fishing village in Mexico surrounded by dry rain forest wilderness is something few can manage. I am continually thankful for such an opportunity. Nonetheless, as described in the last chapter, what I have done to make Nature as all important is feasible in cities too. For the cancer-related goals I use Nature to remind me of that the tumors are a gift in many ways. Once an oak tree had a large tumor on its trunk and I learned how the tumor had saved the tree's life. Baby turtles taught me about taking risks as I watched them leave their nest for the open sea, knowing full well their chances for survival were slim. Movements of stars and the relationship of moon cycles to tides all provide metaphors I can apply to becoming healthier each day. I could go on and on with how I intentionally and consistently mindful about using everything in Nature to help with my goals. Not a day goes by where I do not learn something about handling stress, moving on, staying disciplined, being patient, showing fortitude or fearlessness, etc. from one of the other-than-human life forms around me. (Of course, I also learn from my fellow human creatures who are part of Nature as well though too often I learn from them what not to do.) When I feel the need for a stronger dose of Nature's medicine (beyond the organic vegetable garden and the edible plants that surround me), I make an effort to immerse myself somehow into a Nature experience whenever possible.

Story Two: **Trying to Save the Oceans**

After the publication of my small political booklet, "The Shrimp Habit: How it is Destroying our Oceans and What you Can Do About it," a book I used to stop the building of a large shrimp farm on the Sea of Cortez, an assassination contract was put on me by the owners. My wife and I immediately left our ocean-view home and relocated on the on the mainland on the Pacific Coast. Being aware of Nature and spending much time in the ocean made it obvious years ago that fish were disappearing rapidly in our area along the Costalegre in the state of Jalisco Mexico where I now live, far from the owners of the shrimp farm on the Sea of Cortez. Local fishermen were going further and further out to sea and returning with smaller and smaller fish. Internet research revealed that less than one percent of the world's oceans have marine preserve no-take zones (NTZ) that had proven successful, but that without at least 15% of the ocean having them all fisheries would become depleted by 2048. Using the Medicine Wheel presented in this book for reflection and action based upon it, I initiated actions that may well result to Mexico's CONANP (Comisión Nacional de Áreas Naturales Protegidas) declaring the first national marine park on our Pacific Coast at the village known as Arroyo Seco. Below I explain how I used the Indigenous CAT-FAWN components of Medicine Wheel to move successfully toward this objective. (To read notices about the progression of the entire process, Google "Marine Park Arroyo Seco" or "Marine Park Four Arrows" as I have made continual postings on the website Kickstarter gave us after a successful funding campaign. By the time you read this, we may be close to becoming the first NTZ preserve on the Pacific Coast of Mexico.)

CAT (Trance-Based Learning)

One day in the *initi* (purification lodge), I felt a strong message from the spirits to take action about the diminishing life in the oceans. The spirit of a huge dorado came into the lodge and its presence conveyed an urgent call for help. I had caught a dorado a few weeks earlier. Perhaps what I felt and saw in the darkness was its spirit. In any case, the mandate was clear. I soon traveled to Cabo Pulmo on the Sea of Cortez to learn about its successful NTZ. I saw for myself the remarkable amount of life in the ocean and how the solar-powered village was thriving with eco-tourism. When I returned to my village on the Pacific coast, I commenced trying to convince the fishing cooperatives in my little village of Punta Perula to create a 16 square kilometer NTZ here, but none trusted that the other cooperatives would honor it and felt that if their members did they would be the only ones not benefitting. After more than a year of dead ends using only willful determination, information about how NTZs worked, brochures, meetings, appeals, efforts to start a foundation, etc., I realized I had not utilized the very thing that inspired me to do the work in the first place. How easy it had been to depend only on such things and forget the spirit world!

Coming back to my Indigenous worldview sensibilities, I went into the lodge specifically to pray for guidance. The next day I met a man with a home in Arroyo Seco, a fishing village about 40 minutes from mine. He had heard about my temazcal and healings that had occurred in it. He had a friend in need of help and asked if he could bring her. Several days after he called me and asked if I would come talk to the fishing cooperative at Arroyo Seco about the importance of saving a mangrove in the area. We had talked about my efforts to create an NTZ knew of my efforts to stop a shrimp farm in Kino Bay Mexico three days north and how the Mexican mafia chased me out of town and brought me three days south to where I lived. So he assumed that I specialized in marine conservation which was not the case.

When I arrived at the meeting in Arroyo Seco around 30 Mexican fishermen were arguing vehemently about permit issues. The President of the cooperative interrupted them when he saw me and introduced me as a professor with knowledge of the mangroves. Unsure of what I would say beyond what I had garnered from the Internet the night before, I went into a light trance and before I knew it I was asking everyone to stand so as to send a prayer out to the oceans. The group, as if in trance themselves, all stood solemnly.

Words and the Direction of Sacred Communication

Surprising myself, I said a prayer in Lakota and then took out a Cherokee flute I often carried and played a song. My Spanish being poor (embarrassingly so considering I live in Mexico), perhaps I intuitively thought the Lakota prayer and the Cherokee song would open up a telepathic channel between my audience and me. When everyone sat back down, I began in my kindergarten Spanish to speak. I tried to say that if an NTZ was the main focus and the community became the first on the coast to create an official national marine park NTZ in the ocean where the mangrove drained, Arroyo Seco could be a model for a land-ocean preserve that would bring eco-tourism to the poor village. I spoke about our relatives in the sea and our responsibilities to them and to future generations of the people who lived in the village. All of these things I was saying were unplanned and I sensed that I was communicating at a level beyond the words. People were nodding and agreeing. I knew the spirits were guiding my communication. I spoke with more and more confidence, knowing it was not my words so much as the telepathy that was operating that conveyed my message.

The group voted unanimously to support such an effort.

Fear and the Directions of Courage and Fearlessness

My going to a new place and speaking to a group of fishermen I did not know in a language I could not speak about a topic I about which I had no expertise at the request of a stranger I had only recently met offered grounds for some anxiety. As soon as I felt it however I considered the higher goal of the greater good and mustered up the courage. When the time came for me to speak the courage coupled with my experience in trance work brought me into fearlessness. From this place, the magic manifested itself in the communication at this first meeting and it has continued.

After the meeting I of course needed to learn about how one creates a national marine park in Mexico. I learned that a federal agency known as CONANP had to create a national marine park but any proposal required a university study with a price tag of around 25,000 American dollars. It also required signatures of the entire community. Without going into detail (which is available on the website), suffice it to say I went to Kickstarter and became their first conservation project (I had to use "food" as my category because they had nothing for ocean preservation). We raised all the money from folks around the world; organized meetings in Arroyo Seco to educate everyone about the NTZ and got the necessary signatures. We received the general support of several federal agencies and hired the University of Guadalajara marine biologists to conduct the study that determined the area was perfect for an NTZ. We are now working the politics of a new administration to create the first national marine park on the coast.

What is not described on the website is the fact that ancient Indigenous understandings about trance-based work; fearlessness; sacred communication, self-authorization and spiritual lessons from the ocean and its life have been fundamental to the entire process and continues to be.

Authority and the Direction of Community-Based Self-Authorship

There is a sort of paradox involved when Indigenous orientations to community-based self-authorship is confronted with a system of rigid hierarchy and external authority such as is required to create a national marine park in Mexico. Yet along the way it has been the self-determination of everyone involved with the Arroyo Seco project that has been the driver, sometimes in spite of the power politics at work in governmental agencies. Self-authorship also helps with finding complementarity and cooperation within the hierarchy. Always, however, it is not the self-authorship of individual ego, competition or one-up positioning that makes such independent thinking so powerful but rather the use of independent thinking, courage and communication in pursuit of the common good of the community. This is a key to the Indigenous worldview.

Self-authorship in the service of community is now allowing for back-up strategies in light of political delays that are happening. We have two ideas in mind that call upon such self-authorship. One is to bring in the top journalist in Mexico to write about how remarkable it is that a small fishing community has decided to create a marine park on its shores; that all the high end hotel and resort owners in the area fully support the project and that no government money is needed to create or protect the NTZ because of worldwide donations from Internet fund-sharing, etc.. Without saying anything negative about government delays or politics, we think this might inspire positive action.

If it does not, another self-authorized action in behalf of community is on the table. It is the possibility of creating a private sanctuary that would have no legal standing. The effort to keep people from fishing or diving in the area would be strictly educational with no enforcement of fines for violators. Most people think such a plan could not work and that fishermen up and down the coast learned about the large stocks of fish and big lobsters, they would laugh at the request to voluntarily leave the area alone. However all along we have been creating education programs aimed at making the place a sacred spot in behalf of future benefits for all. It might work and bring even more people to Arroyo Seco.

Nature and the Direction of Nature is All

From the moment the spirit of the dorado came into the lodge to ask for help, the spiritual energies of ocean, coastal and inland landscapes has continued to inspire the remarkable synchronicities and successful outcomes of the project. In concert with observable and researchable knowledge about how small "no take zones" every 40 kilometers or so could rapidly bring fisheries back into balance, the sea turtles, pelicans, fish and the ocean waves all continue to offer lessons for how to proceed with this task. For example, one day I was paddling with someone with some potential influence and trying to convince him to help with promoting the project. At one crucial point in the conversation where I was talking about how much our fellow ocean creatures need our help, two large dorados swam just under the surface side by side between our two boards less than 50 meters off shore. Matter-of-factly, I said to my amazed friend that the pair of beautiful green and blue fish came to support what I was saying. He made his mind up on the spot to help out. This unusual event is one of many I could describe to show how the inspiration and teachings of Nature can guide us.

References

Preface

Gill, Jerry H. *Native American worldviews: An introduction*. New York, NY: Humanity Press, 2002. Print.

Johansen, Bruce E. "Adventures in Denial: Ideologial Resistance to the Idea that the Iroquoise Helped Shape American Democracy." *Unlearning the Language of Conquest: Scholars Expose Anti-Indianism in America*. Ed. Four Arrows. Austin: University of Texas Press, 2008. Print.

LaFrance, Brenda E., and James E. Costello. "Reinforcing the Three Principles of Goodmindedness, Peacefulness, and Strength to Protect the Natural World." *Preserving Tradition and Understanding the Past: Papers from the Conference on Iroquois Research, 2001–2005*. Ed. Christine Sternberg Patrick. New York, NY: The University of the State of New York, 2010. Web.

Little Bear, Leroy. "Jagged worldviews collide." *Reclaiming Indigenous voice and vision*. Ed. M. Battiste. Vancouver: UBC Press, 2000. 77–85. Print.

Ransom, James W., and Kreg Ettenger. "Polishing the Kaswentha: A Haudenosaunee View of Environmental Cooperation." *Environmental Science and Policy*. 1987.4 (4–5): 219–228. Web.

Walker, Polly O. "Decolonizing Conflict Resolution." *American Indian Quarterly*. 29 (3&4). 527–549. Print.

Weatherford, Jack. *Indian Givers: How the Indians of the Americas Transformed the World*. New York, NY: Fawcett Columbine, 1988. Print.

Point of Departure, pages 155–167
Copyright © 2016 by Information Age Publishing

Introduction

Abram, David. *Becoming Animal: An Earthly Cosmology.* New York, NY: Pantheon, 2010. Print.

Alford, Dan Moonhawk. "Manifesting Worldviews in Language." n.d. Web.

Axelrod, Robert. *The Evolution of Cooperation.* NY: Basic Books, 1984. Print.

"Episode 8: Rupert Sheldrake." Campbell, Duncan. *Living Dialogues.* n.d. Web.

Ceballos, Geraldo, et al. "Accelerated modern human–induced species losses: Entering the sixth mass extinction." *Science Advances* 1.5 (2015). Print.

Darwin, Charles. *The Descent of Man.* 1879. Murray, John, Charles Moore, and Adrian Desmond. New York, NY: Penguin, 2004. Kindle.

Davidson-Hunt, Iain., and Fikret Berkes. "Changing Resource Management Paradigms, Traditional Ecological Knowledge, and Non-timber Forest Products." *Forest Communities in the Third Millennium: Linking Research, Business, and Policy toward a Sustainable Non-timber Forest Product Sector, Proceedings of the meeting.* Ed. L. C. Duchesne, J. C. Zasada. Kenora. Web. December 13, 2015.

Deloria, Philip J. *Playing Indian.* New Haven: Yale University Press. Print.

Eisler, Rian. *The Chalice and the Blade: Our History, Our Future.* San Francisco, CA: Harper and Row, 1987. Print.

Elias, Dean. "It's time to change our minds: An introduction to transformative learning." *ReVision.* ReVision, 27 June 1997. Web.

Fabbro, David. "Peaceful Societies: An Introduction." *Journal of Peace Research* 15.1 (1978): 67–83. Print.

Fleming, Steven. M. *Scientific American Mind,* 25 (2014): 30–37. Print.

Four Arrows, Greg Cajete, and John Lee. *Critical Neurophilosophy and Indigenous Wisdom.* Netherlands: Sense Publications, 2013. Print.

Four Arrows, Ed. *Unlearning the Language of Conquest: Scholars Expose Anti-Indianism in America.* 2008. Austin: University of Texas Press. Print.

Four Arrows. "The Continuing Saga of Anti-Indianism in America: Critique of a Bestseller and the Reviewers Who Praise it." *Truthout.* 12 October 2014. Web.

Gabriel, Richard A. "The Archaeology of War," *The Culture of War: Invention and Early Development.* Ed. Gabriel, Richard. Westport: Greenwood, 1990. 19-3. Print.

Hampton, Chris, Bill Berkowitz, and Kate Nagy. "Developing Baseline Measures of Behavior." *Community Toolbox,* N.D. Web..

Hans, Lew. C. *Self-awareness- An Emerging Field in Neurobiology.* Ed. Acta Paediatrica. 4.2: 121–122. Web.

Hedlund-de Witt, Annick. *Worldviews and the Transformation to Sustainable Societies.* Doctoral dissertation, 2013. Web.

Horse, Perry. G. "Native American Identity." *New Directions for Student Services,* 2005.109, 61–68.

Hufana, Leialani. "Interating Traditional Ecological Knowledge with Modern Day Ecosystem Management and Restoration Practices." Master's Thesis. University of San Francisco, 2014. Web.

Isquith, Elias "We're in a Revolutionary Moment: Why Chris Hedges Believes the Uprising is Coming Soon," 2011 Occupy.Com Interview. Web.

Jacobs, Don Trent. "On Being Indian." Red Ink. Journal of the American Indian Studies Program. 2001. University of Arizona. Print.

Kelly, Alexia, and Stefan Raubenheimer. *Green Growth in Practice*, 2014. Web.

Kimmerer, Robin Wall. *Braiding Sweetgrass: Indigenous Wisdom, Scientific Knowledge and the Teachings of Plants.* Minneapolis: Milkweed Editions, 2013. Print.

Leakey, Richard and Roger Lewin, Eds. *People of the Lake: Mankind and Its Beginnings.* Garden City: Anchor/Doubleday, 1978. Print.

Leakey, Richard E. and Roger Lewin. *Origins: What New Discoveries Reveal about the Emergence of Our Species.* London: Macdonald and Janes, 1990. Print.

Lewellen, Ted C. "The Evolution of the State" *Political Anthropology*. Ed. Ted C. Lewellen South Hadley: Bergin and Garvey, 2003. 41-62. Web.

Levy, Paul. *Dispelling Wetico: Breaking the Curse of Evil.* Berkeley: North Atlantic Press, 2013. Print.

Lifshitz, Michael, and Amir Raz. "Hypnotic Ability and Baseline Attention" *Psychology of Consciousness: Theory, Research and Practice.* 2.2 (2015): 134–143. Web.

Looking Horse, Arvol et al. "Proclamation on Protection of Ceremonies." Indian Country Today, 2003 Web.

Mesteth, Wilmer, Darrell Standing Elk, and Phyllis Swift Hawk. "War Against Exploiters of Lakota Spirituality." 1998. Web.

Milman, Oliver. "James Hansen, father of climate change awareness, calls Paris talks 'a fraud'." *The Guardian*, 12 December 2015. Web.

Narvaez, Darcia. "The 99 Percent–Development and Socialization within an Evolutionary Context: Growing Up to Become 'A Good and Useful Human Being.'" *War, Peace and Human Nature: The Convergence of Evolutionary and Cultural Views.* Ed. D. Fry. New York, NY: Oxford University Press, 2010. 643-672. Print.

Narvaez, Darcia. *Neurobiology and the Development of Human Morality: Evolution, Culture and Wisdom.* New York, NY: W.W. Norton, 2014. Print.

Owen, Suzanne. *The Appropriation of Native American Spirituality.* New York, NY: Continuum International publishing Group, 2008. Print.

Perkins, John. *Shapeshifting: Techniques for Global and Personal Transformation.* Springfield, Mass: Destiny Press, 1997. Print.

Ravven, H. M. *The self beyond itself: An alternative history of ethics, the new brain sciences, and the myth of free will.* New York, NY: New Press, 2013. Print.

Redfield, R. *Peasant society and culture: An anthropological approach to civilization.* Chicago: University of Chicago Press, 1956. Print.

Redfield, Robert *The Primitive world and its Transformations*. Ithaca: Cornell University Press, 1953. Print.

Schlitz, Marilyn, et al. "The Worldview Literacy Project: Exploring New Capacities for the 21st Century Student." *New Horizons for Learning*, Johns Hopkins University School of Education, Winter (2011): IX, 1. Web.

Shepard, Paul. *Coming Home to the Pleistocene*. Ed. Florence R. Shepard. Washington, D.C.: Island Press, 1998.

Smedley. *Race in North America: Origin and Evolution of a Worldview*. 3rd ed. Boulder: Westview Press, 2007. Print.

Snow, William Parker. "A Few Remarks on the Wild Tribes of Tierra del Fuego from Personal Observation," *Transactions of the Ethnological Society of London* 1 (1861): 261–67. Print.

Sponsel, Leslie E. "The Natural history of peace: The positive View of Human Nature and its Potential" *A Natural History of Peace*. Ed. Gregor, Thomas. Nashville: Vanderbilt University Press, 1996. Print.

Stanford University. "Sixth mass extinction is here: Humanity's existence threatened" *ScienceDaily*, 19 June 2015. Web.

Tarnis, Richard. *Cosmos and Psyche: Intimations for a New Worldview*. New York, NY: Plume Publishers, 1997. Print.

Wilco, John C. *Robert Redfield and the development of American anthropology*. Oxford: Lexington Books, 2004. Print.

Worm, Boris, et al. "Impacts of Biodiversity Loss on Ocean Ecosystem Services." *Science* 314. (2006): 787–790.

Wildcat, Daniel. *Red Alert! Saving the Planet with Indigenous Knowledge*. Golden: Fulcrum Publishing, 2009. Print.

Wilshire, Bruce "On the Very Idea of 'A Worldview' and of 'Alternative Worldviews'" *Unlearning the Language of Conquest: Scholars Expose Anti-Indianism in America*. Ed. Four Arrows. Austin: University of Texas Press, 2008. Print.

Chapter 1

Aizenstein, H. J., et al. "Complementary category learning systems identified using event-related functional MRI." *Journal of Cognitive Neuroscience*, 12.6 (2000): 977–987. Print.

Amoss, P. *Coast Salish spirit dancing*. Seattle: University of Washington Press. 1978. Print.

Askay, S. W., D. R. Patterson, and S. R. Sharar. Virtual reality hypnosis. *Contemporary Hypnosis* 26.1 (2009): 40–47. Print.

Atkinson, J. *Trauma trails, recreating song lines: The transgenerational effects of trauma in Indigenous Australia*. North Melbourne: Spinifex. 2002. Print.

Benson, H. *Timeless healing: The power and biology of belief*. New York, NY: Scribner. (1996). Print.

Budzynskiu, Thomas. "The clinical guide to sound and light." *Stanford*. Stanford University, 6 Dec. 2015. Web.

Dagmar Zeithamova, M. A. "Category Learning Systems" *Dissertation.* Austin: University of Texas, 2008. Print.

Doak, Bridget. "Effects of shamanic drumming on anxiety, mood, states of consciousness, imagery, and brain patterns in adult subjects." *Dissertation abstracts international* 67.9-A (2007): 3215. Web.

Draganski, Bogdan, et al. "Neuroplasticity: changes in grey matter induced by training." *Nature* 427 (2004): 311–312. Web.

Four Arrows, D., G. Cajete, and J. Lee. *Critical neurophilosophy and Indigenous wisdom.* Rotterdam: Sense Publishing, 2010. Print.

Gilligan, Stephen. "Three Minds and Three Levels of Consciousness: A Self Relations Framework for Generative Trance." *Stephen Gilligan.com blog.* Web.

Green, Elmer, and Alice M. Green. "Biofeedback and States of Consciousness," *Handbook of States of Consciousness* Ed. B. B. Wolman & M. Ullman.. New York, NY: Van Van Nosttrand Reinhold Company, 1986. Print.

Jacobs, Don. "Calm Training for a Wild Mustang Horseman." *Horseman Magazine.* 1986. Print.

Jacobs, Donald Trent. *Patient Communication for First Responders: The First Hour of Trauma.* Englewood Cliffs: Prentice-Hall (Brady), 1998. Print.

Jeans, Sir James. "The Mysterious Universe." *Wikiquotes.* New York, NY: Pelican Books, 1937. Web.

Jung, Carl. G. *Jung on Active Imagination.* Ed. Joseph Chodorow. Princeton, NJ: Princeton University Press, 1997. Print.

Kaptchuck, Ted J. "Intentional ignorance: a history of blind assessment and placebo controls in medicine." *Bulletin of the history of medicine* 72.3 (1998): 389–433. Print.

Kaufman, Roan. *How Might the Ayahuasca Experience be a Potential Antidote to Western Hegemony: A Mixed Methods Study.* Diss. Fielding Graduate University. Proquest Dissertations Publishing, 2015. Print.

Kosslyn, Stephen M., William L. Thompson, Maria F. Constantini-Ferrando, Nathaniel M. Alper and David Spiegel, "Hypnotic Visual Illusion Alters Color Processing in the Brain," in *American Journal of Psychiatry,* 2000, 157: 1279-1284. Web.

Levy, Paul. *Dispelling Wetico: Breaking the Curse of Evil,* 2013. Berkeley,CA: North Atlantic Press. Print

Luders, Eileen, T, et al. "The underlying anatomical correlates of long-term meditation: larger hippocampal and frontal volumes of gray matter." *Neuroimage* 45 (2008): 672–678. Print.

Maybury-Lewis, David. *Millennium: Tribal Wisdom and the Modern World.* New York, NY: Viking, 1992. Print.

Makuuchi, M., Kaminago, and T. Sugishita. "Brain Activation During Ideomotor Praxis: Imitation and Movements Executive by Verbal Command" *Journal of Neurosurgery Psychiatry.* 76 (2005). 25–33. Print.

Nemeth, Dezco, et al. "Boosting Human Learning by Hypnosis," *Cerebral Cortex* 801-5 (23 April 2013). PubMed. Web.

Nauwald, Nana. "Trance." *Ritual Body Postures*, Ecstatic Trance, nd. Web.

Peat, David. *Blackfoot Physics: A Journey into the Native American Universe*. London: Fourth Estate, 1994. Print.

Ri, Joo-yeon Christina. *The Last Leaf: A Triangulated Study of a "Sights and Sounds of Nature" Film as a Motivator for Ecologically Sustainable Practices*. Diss. Fielding Graduate University, 2008. Proquest Dissertations. Print.

Rossi, Ernest L., and Kathryn L. Rossi. "The Neuroscience of Observing Consciousness & Mirror Neurons in Therapeutic Hypnosis." *American Journal of Clinical Hypnosis* 48:4 (April 2006). Print.

Rothman, Kenneth J., and Karen B. Michels. "The continuing unethical use of placebo controls," *New England Journal of Medicine 331*.6 (1994): 394–398. Print.

Sorenson, E. Richard. "Preconquest Consciousness." *Tribal Epistemologies: Essays in the Philosophy of Anthropology*. Ed. Helmut Wautischer. London: Ashgate, 2003. 79–115. Print.

Thomason, Timothy C. "The Role of Altered States of Consciousness in Native American Healing." *Journal of Rural Community Psychology* E3.1 (2010): 44–56. Print.

Villoldo, Albero, and Stanley Krippner. *The Realms of Healing*. New York, NY: Simon & Schuster, 1987. Print.

Walsh, Roger. *The World of Shamanism*. New York, NY: Llewellyn Publications, 2007. Print.

Williams, Mike. *Prehistoric Belief: Shamans, Trance and the Afterlife*. Stroud: Great Britain: The History Press, 2010. Print.

Yasuo, Shigenori Nagatomo, and Monte S. Hull. *The Body, Self-Cultivation, and Ki-Energy*. Albany: State University of New York Press, 1993. Print.

Chapter 2

Altamirano-Jimenez, I. *Indigenous Encounters with Neoliberalism, Place, Women and the Environment in Canada and Mexico*. Vancouver, BC: University of British Columbia Press. Print.

American Academy of Orthopedic Surgeons. *Care and Transportation of the Sick and Injured*. Sudberry, MA: Jones and Bartlett, 2013. Print.

Anthropology Outreach Office. *Smithsonian Institution: A Critical Bibliography on North American Indians*, 2013. Web.

Benton-Banai, Edward. *The Mishomis Book: The Voice of the Ojibway*. Minnesota: University of Minnesota Press, 2010. Print.

Bhola, H. S. "Reclaiming Old Heritage for Proclaiming Future History: The Knowledge for Development Debate in African Contexts." *Africa Today* 49.3 (2002): 3–21. Print.

Bower, Brett. "War arose recently, anthropologists contend" *Science News*, 2013, Web.

Brown, Dee. *Bury My Heart at Wounded Knee: An Indian History of the American West.* New York, NY: Holt & Co., 1991. Print.

Chomsky Noam. *What Uncle Sam Really Wants.* Tucson, AZ: Odonian Press, 1992. Print.

Chomsky, Noam quoted in Keefer, M. "Noam Chomsky: Indigenous people are the ones taking the lead in trying to protect all of us." *The Two Row Times.* 5 Nov. 2013. Web.

Chomsky, Noam, Lois Meyer, and Benjamin Maldonado Alvarado. *Noam Chomsky Voices from North, South, and Central America.* San Francisco, CA: City Lights Books. Web.

Cox, James. L. *The Invention of God in Indigenous Societies.* New York, NY: Routledge, 2014. Print.

Davis, July L. *Survival Schools: The American Indian Movement and Community Education in the Twin Cities.* Minneapolis, MN: University of Minnesota Press, 2013. Print.

Devadatta Kali Jaya "Native American Spirituality: A Vedantic View." *Vandata. org.* 2005. Web.

Four Arrows. "Resistance at the Roots." *School Against Neoliberal Rule: Educational Fronts for Local and Global Justice: A Reader.* Eds. Abendroth, Mark and Brad Porfilio. Charlotte: Information Age Publishing, 2015. Print.

Gandhi, Mahatma. "Mind of Mahatma Gandhi," *Encyclopedia of Gandhi's Thoughts.* 1960. Eds. Acharya Vinoba Bhave and S. Radhakrishnan. Ahemadabad: Jitendrat T. Desai. 1969. Web.

Global Witness. *Deadly Environment Report.* 2014. Web.

Jaynes, Julian. *The Origin of Consciousness in the Breakdown of the Bicameral Mind.* New York, NY: Houghton Mifflin, 1976. Print.

Kujur, Joseph Marianus "Gandhian thought Vis-V-Vis Indigenous Ideology." *The Meaning of Mahatma for the Millennium.* Ed. Kurivilla Pandikattu Gandhi. Washington, D.C.: Council for Research in Values and Philosophy, 2001. 83–92. Web.

Leavitt, G. C. "The Frequency of Warfare: An Evolutionary Perspective." *Sociol Inquiry* 47 (1997): 49-58. Web.

Mann, Barbara Alice. "Where are Your Women?" *Unlearning the Language of Conquest: Scholars Expose Anti-Indianism in America.* Ed. Four Arrows. Austin, TX: University of Texas Press. Print.

Maybury-Lewis, David. *Millennium: Tribal wisdom and the modern world.* New York, NY: Penguin, 1992. Print.

McGaa, Ed (Eagle Man). *Rainbow Tribe: Ordinary People Journeying on the Red Road.* New York, NY: Harper, 1992. Print.

Mosha, R. Sambuli. *The Heartbeat of Indigenous Africa: A Study of the Chagga Educational System.* London: Routledge, 2000. Print.

Nash, Paul. *Authority and Freedom in Education.* New York, NY: John Wiley and Sons, 1966. Print.

Palmer, Parker. *The Courage to Teach: Exploring the Inner Landscapes of a Teachers Life*. San Francisco, CA: Jossey-Bass, 2007. Print.

Self. Best Bodies. Web.

Smith, Huston and Gary Rhine. *A Seat at the Table: In Conversation with Native Americans*, 2006: Berkeley, CA: University of California Berkeley Press. Print.

Smith, Huston. *Forgotten Truth*. 1992. San Francisco, CA: HarperCollins. Print.

Smith, Huston. *The World's Religions*. New York, NY: HarperCollins, 1958. Print.

Stokes, Stephen. *Philosophy: 100 essential thinkers*. London: Arcturus Publishing Limited. Print.

Van der Dennen, J. M. G. *The origin of war: The evolution of a male-coalitional reproductive strategy*. 2 vols. San Rafael, CA: Origin Press, 2009. Print.

Veeravali, Anuradha. *Gandhi in Political Theory: Truth, Law and Experiment*. Burlington: Ashgate Publishing Limited, 2014. Print.

Veeravalli, Anuradha. *Gandhi in Political Theory: Truth, Law and Experiment*. Burlington, VT; Ashgate Publishing Limited, 1988. Print.

Woodruff, Paul. *Citizen Socrates: 5th Annual Platsis Symposium*. Ann Arbor: University of Michigan, Sept. 29, 2006. Web.

Chapter 3

Bauerlein, Mark. *The Dumbest Generation: How the Digital Age Stupefies our Young Americans and Jeopardizes our Future*. New York, NY: Tarcher/Penguin, 2008. Print.

Baxter-Magold, Marcia. "Epistemological Reflection: The Evolution of Epistemological Assumptions." *Personal Epistemology: The Psychology of Beliefs about Knowledge and Knowing*. Eds. B. K. Hofer and P. R. Pintrich. Mahwah, NJ: Lawrence Erlaum. Print.

Boehm, Christopher, et al. "Egaliararian Behavior and Reverse Dominance Hierarchy" *Current Anthropology* 34.3 (1993): 227–254. Print.

Deloria, Jr. Vine, and Daniel R. Wildcat. *Power and Place: Indian Education in America*. Golden: Fulcrum Resources. Print.

Eqeiq, Amal. "Writing the Indigenous: Contemporary Mayan Literature in Chiapas, Mexico and Palestinian Literature in Israel." Diss. U of Washington, 2013. Print.

Ermine, Willie. "Aboriginal epistemology." *First Nations Education in Canada*. Eds. M. Battiste and J. Barman. Vancouver: UBC Press, 1995. 101–112. Print.

Fannin, Jeffrey & Williams, Rob. "Leading Edge Neuroscience Reveals Significant Correlations Between Beliefs, The Whole-Brain State and Psychotherapy" *CQ: The CAPA Quarterly*. Counseling and Psychological Association of New South Wales. 2012. Pg 14–18. Web.

Fromm, Erich. *To Have or to Be?* New York, NY: Continuum Publishing, 1976. Print.

Gelbspan, Ross. *The Heat is On.* New York, NY: Perseus Book, 1997. Print.

Godelier, Maurice. *The Making of Great Men: Male Domination and Power Among the New Guinea Baruya.* Cambridge, GM: Cambridge University Press, 1986. Print.

Gray, Peter. "How Hunter Gatherers Maintained Their Egalitarian Ways." *Psychology Today* Web.

Gross, Lawrence W. *Anishinaabe Ways of Knowing and Being.* London: Ashbate Publishing, Ltd., 2014. Print.

Hart, Michael Anthony. "Indigenous Worldviews, Knowledge, and Research: The Development of an Indigenous Research Paradigm." *Journal of Indigenous Voices in Social Work.* 1.1 (Feb. 2010). Print.

Highwater, Jamake. *The Primal Mind: Vision and Reality in Indian America.* New York, NY: Meridian, 1992. Print.

Kenyon, Chris and Stewart Hase. "Moving from Andragogy to Heutagogy in Vocational Education." *Research to Reality: Putting VET Research to Work.* Eric. Print.

Lee, Richard B. "Reflections on primitive communism." *Hunters and Gatherers: History, Evolution, and Culture Change.* Eds. Tim Ingold, David C. Riches, and James C. Woodburn. Oxford: Berg. 1988. 252–268. Print.

Lincoln, Kenneth, Indi'n Humor. *Bicultural Play in Native America.* Oxford University Press, 1993. Print.

McKenzie, Brad, and Vern Morrissette. "Social work practice with Canadians of Aboriginal Background: Guidelines for Respectful Social Work." *Multicultural Social Work in Canada: Working with Diverse Ethno-racial Communities.* Eds. A. Al-Krenawi and J. R. Graham. Ontario: Oxford University Press. 2003. 251-282. Print.

Reyhner, Jon and Jeanne Eder. "American Indian Education: A History." *History of Education Quarterly.* 45.1 (Spring, 2005): 146–148. Print.

Ri, Jooyeon Christina. *The Last Leaf: A Triangulated Study of Sights and Sounds of Nature.* Santa Barbara: Fielding Graduate University, 2008. Print.

Shenkman, Richard. *Just How Stupid Are We? Facing the Truth About the American Voter.* New York, NY: Basic Books. Print.

Simpson, Leanne . "Anishinaabe ways of Knowing." *Aboriginal Health, Identity and Resources* Eds. J. Oakes, R. Riew, S. Koolage, L. Simpson, and N. Schuster. Winnipeg: Native Studies Press, 2000. 165–185. Web.

Szegedy-Maszak, Marianne. "The Secret Mind: How Your Unconscious Really Shapes Your Decisions." *US News & World Report.* US News, 28 Feb. 2005. 53–61. Web.

Wason, Paul. K. *The Archaeology of Rank.* Cambridge, UK: Cambridge University Press, 1994. Print.

Chapter 4

Blench, Roger. *Archeology, Language and the African Past.* Lanham: AltaMira Press, 2007. Print.

Bok, Sissela. L*ying: Moral Choice in Public and Private Life.* New York, NY: Vintage Books, 1999. Print.

Bronson, Matthew C. "Lessons in the Old Language" *Global Oneness Project.* N.D. Web.

Cajete, Greg. *Look to the Mountain: An Ecology of Indigenous Education.* Durango, CO: Kivaki Press, 1994. Print.

Camacho, Jose, et al. *Information Structure in Indigenous Languages of the Americas: Syntactic Approaches.* Berlin: De Gruyter Mouton, 2010. Web.

Cook, Eung-Do, and Darin Flynn. "Aboriginal Languages of Canada" *Contemporary Linguistic Analysis: An Introduction,* 6th ed. Eds. O'Grady. W and D Archibald. Toronto: Pearson Langman, 2008. Print.

Cooper, Thomas W. A. *Time Before Deceptio:. Truth in Communication, Culture and Ethics.* Sante Fe: Clear Light Publishers, 1998. Print.

Cordón, Luis A. *Popular Psychology: An Encyclopedia.* Westport: Greenwood Press, 2005. Web.

de Villiers, Jill. "The Interface of Language and Theory of Mind." *Lingua.* 117:11. Nov. 2007. Web.

Debey, Evelyne, Maarten De Schryver, Gordon D. Logan, et al. "From Junior to Senior Pinocchio: a Cross-sectional Lifespan Investigation of Deception." *ACTA PSYCHOLOGICA* 160 (2015): 58–68. Print.

Deloria, Jr. Vine, and Daniel R. Wildcat. *Power and Place: Indian Education in America.* Golden: American Indian Graduate Center and Fulcrum Resources, 2001. Print.

Doherty, Lillian Eileen. *Homer's Odyssey.* New York, NY: Oxford University Press, 2009. Print.

Eisner, Eliot W. *The Arts and the Creation of Mind.* New Haven: Yale University Press, 2002. Print.

Ford-Smith, H. (1987). *Lionheart Gal: Life stories of Jamaican women.* Toronto: Sister Vision, 2005. Print.

Four Arrows, and Walter Block. *Differing Worldviews in Higher Education: Two Scholars Argue Cooperatively about Justice Education.* The Netherlands: Sense Publishing, 2011. Print.

Gentner, Dedre, and Lera Boroditsky. "Early Acquisition of Nouns and Verbs: Evidence from Navajo." *Routes to Language.* Web.

Gentner, Dedre. "Why nouns are learned before verbs: Linguistic relativity versus natural partitioning. In Language development" *Vol. 2: Language, thought and culture.* Ed. Stan A. Kuczaj. Hillsdale: Erlbaum,1997, 301–304. Web.

Gray, Russell D., and Quentin D. Atkinson. "Language-tree Divergence Times Support the Anatolian Theory of Indo-European Origin." *Nature.* Aug. 2003. Web.

Jacobs, Don Trent. *Primal Awareness: A True Story of Survival, Transformation and Awakening with the Raramuri Shamans of Mexico.* Rochester: Inner Traditions International, 1998. Print.

Hesse, Herman. *Wandering: Notes and Sketches.* New York, NY: Farrar, Straus & Giroux, 1972. Print.

Keyes, Ralph. *The Post-Truth Era: Dishonesty and Deception in Contemporary Life.* New York, NY: Martin Press, 2004. Print.

Kindler, Anna M. "Art as a Language for Communication and Critical Awareness (Or Not?)". n.d. Web.

Kipling, Rudyard. "Surgeons of the Soul." *Book of Words.* Adeline University Press. 1928. Web.

Lawlor, Robert. *Voices of the First Day.* Rochester: Inner Traditions International, 1991. Print.

Lewis, M. Paul, Gary F. Simons, and Charles D. Fennig. *Ethnologue: Languages of the World.* 17th ed. Dallas: SIL International, 2013. Print.

Li, Peggy, Linda Abarbanell, Lila Gleitman, and Anna Papgragou. "Spatial Reasoning in Tenejapan Mayans." *Cognition.* April, 2011. Web.

Litman, Robert J. *The Greek Experiment: Imperialism and Social Conflict 800-400 BC.* New York, NY: Harcourt College Publishers, 1974. Print.

Little Bear, Leroy. *Dialogues Between Indigenous and Western Scientists.* Kalamazoo: Fetzer Institute, 1992. Print.

Lucy, John A. "The Sapir-Whorf Hypothesis." *Routledge Encyclopedia of Philosophy.* Ed. Craig Edward. London: Routledge, 1998. Print.

Mahaffey, J. P. *The Greek World Under Roman Sway.* London: Macmillan, 1890. Print.

Mihas, Elena, Bernard Perley, Gabriel Rei-Doval, and Kathleen Wheatley. "Responses to language endangerment. In honor of Mickey Noonan." *Studies in Language Companion Series 142.* Amsterdam: John Benjamins. (2013). 3–19. Print.

O'Flaherty, Wendy D. *Dreams, Illusions and Other Realities.* Chicago: University of Chicago Press, 1984. Print.

Ogura, T., et al. "The use of nouns and verbs by Japanese children and their caregivers in book-reading and toy-playing contexts." *Journal of Child Language,* 33 (2006): 1–29. Web.

Ostler, Rosemary. "Disappearing Languages." *Whole Earth,* 2000. Web.

Peat, David F. *Blackfoot Physics: A Journey into the Native American Universe.* London: Fourth Estate Limited, 1994. Print.

Peat, David F. *Synchronicity: The Bridge Between Matter and Mind.* New York, NY: Bantam, 1988. Print.

Pfeiler, Barbara Blaha. *Learning Indigenous Languages: Child Language Acquisition in Mesoamerica.* Boston, MA: Walter de Gruyter, 2007. Print.

Rieber, Robert W. "Dialogues on the Psychology of Language and Thought." 1983. Web.

Ross, Allen C. *Mitakuye Oyasin.* Denver: Wiconi Waste, 1998. Print.

Shore, Cecilia. *Individual Differences in Language Development.* Thousand Oaks: Sage Pub, 1995. Web.

Smith, Huston. *Why Religion Matters: The Fate of the Human Spirit in an Age of Disbelief.* HarperCollins, 2003. EBook. Web.

Sobrevila, Claudia. *The Role of Indigenous Peoples in Biodiversity Conservation: The Natural but Often Forgotten Partners.* Washington: The International Bank for Reconstruction and Development/The World Banks. 2008. Web.

Spence, Sean, Tom F. D. Farrow, Amy E. Herford, et al. "Behavioral and Functional Anatomical Correlates of Deception in Humans." *NeuroReport.* 12.13 (2001): 2849–2853. Print.

Tuting, Alfred W. "Some Reflections on Lakota Language Structures" n.p. Web.

Warrior, Robert. *The World of Indigenous North America.* London: Routledge, 2014. Print.

Chapter 5

Blondin, George. *Yamoria The Lawmaker: Stories of the Dene.* Edmonton: New West Publishers Inc., 1997. Print.

Brown, Joseph Epes. *Animals of the Soul: Sacred Animals of the Oglala Sioux.* Rockport: Element Press, 1997. Print.

Cohen, Michael J. *The Web of Life Imperative: Regenerative Ecopsychology Techniques.* Vancouver: Trafford Publishing, 2003. Print.

Eastman, Charles A. *Indian Scout Craft and Lore.* New York, NY: Dover Publications, 1974. Print.

Eastman, Charles Alexander (Ohiyesa). *The Soul of the Indian: An Interpretation.* Lincoln: Bison Books and University of Nebraska Press. 1980. Print.

Four Arrows (Sept. 2014) "False doctrine and the stifling of Indigenous political will" *Critical Education.* 5.13. Web.

Game, David. *D. H. Lawrence's Australia: Anxiety at the Edge of Empire.* New York, NY: Ashgate Publishing, 2015. Print.

Graham, Mary "Some Thoughts about the Philosophical Underpinnings of Aboriginal Worldviews." *Worldviews: Global Religions, Culture and Ecology.* 3.2 (1999). 105–108. Print.

Harrison, Regina. "Signs, songs, and memory in the Andes: Translating Quechua language and culture" University of West Michigan. Web.

Kimmerer, Robin Wall. *Braiding Sweetgrass: Indigenous Wisdom, Scientific Knowledge and the Teachings of Plants.* Minneapolis: Milkweed Editions, 2013. Print.

King, Thomas. *All my Relations: An Anthology of Contemporary Canadian Native Fiction.* Toronto: McClelland & Stewart, 1990. Print.

King, Thomas. *The Truth About Stories: A Native Narrative.* Toronto: House of Anansi Press, 2003. Print.

Lawrence, D. H. *A Propos of Lady Chatterley's Lover.* New York, NY: Penguin Books, 1961. Print.

Linder, Douglas O. "The Dakota Conflict Trials." Web.

Lopenzina, Drew. "'Good Indian': Charles Eastman and the Warrior as Civil Servant." *American Indian Quarterly* 27 (2003): 3–4. 727–57. Web.

Mann, Barbara Alice. *Spirits of Blood, Spirits of Breath: The Twinned Cosmos of Indigenous America.* New York, NY: Oxford University Press, 2016. Print.

Martinez, David. *Dakota Philosopher: Charles Eastman and American Indian Thought.* St Paul: Minnesota Historical Society, 2009. Print.

Rothbard, Murray N. "The 'Rights' of Animals." *Mises Daily.* Mises Institute of Autraian Economics, Freedom and Peace. 2007. Web.

Sayre, Robert F. *Thoreau and the American Indians.* Princeton: Princeton University Press, 1977. Print.

Smagorinsky, Peter, and Joel Taxel. *The Discourse of Character Education: Culture Wars in the Classroom.* Mahwah: Lawrence Erlbaum Associates, Publishers, 2005. Print.

Spaulding, Roderick J. *An Alternative Expert Knowledge Transfer Model: A Case Study of an Indigenous Storytelling Approach.* Ed. D. Dissertation, Fielding Graduate University. ProQuest. Print.

Warrior, Robert Allen. "Canaanites, Cowboys and Indians: Deliverance, Conquest and Liberation Theology Today" *Christianity and Crisis* 1 (1989). Print.

Warrior, Robert Allen. *Tribal Secrets: Recovering American Indian Intellectual Traditions.* Minneapolis: University of Minnesota Press, 1995. Print.

Webb, Hilary. "The Splendid and the Savage: The Dance of the Opposites in Indigenous Andean Thought." *Journal of Transpersonal Psychology* 4 (March, 2013): 69–83. Web.

Wilson, Raymond. *Ohiyesa: Charles Eastman, Santee Sioux.* Urbana: University of Illinois Press, 1983. Print.

Printed in Great Britain
by Amazon